The
Thinking
Toolbox

The Thinking Toolbox

Thirty-Five Lessons
That Will Build Your
Reasoning Skills

by Nathaniel Bluedorn
& Hans Bluedorn
illustrated by Richard LaPierre

July 2005
CHRISTIAN LOGIC

The Thinking Toolbox
by Nathaniel Bluedorn and Hans Bluedorn

Library of Congress Control Number: 2005901223
ISBN 0-9745315-1-0

Christian Logic
P.O. Box 46
Muscatine, Iowa 52761
309-537-3464
www.christianlogic.com

"…Thou shalt not steal,…Thou shalt love thy neighbour as thyself." – Romans 13:9 "Thou shalt not muzzle the ox that treadeth out the corn. And, The labourer is worthy of his reward." – 1 Timothy 5:18

Though you look, and look, and look,
among the tools inside this book,
you'll find no crescent wrench,
nor hammer for your bench.
For though this book will not repair your sink,
it may teach you how to think.
— *Toodles*

Contents

4 Tools for Science

5 Projects

6 Answer Key

Introduction

How to Use This Book

We hope this book is so easy to use that we don't need to explain anything.

But we suspect our printer may secretly fill these pages with incredibly boring stuff on logic, instead of the gripping mystery this book should contain. So here are a few hints on how to use our book to learn logic, just in case this happens.

The Thinking Toolbox is for anyone aged thirteen through adult. Our previous book, *The Fallacy Detective,* is an easy start to logic. We wrote both books to work well together.

Adults and Children at Home

You can read this book by yourself, or you can read it with others. Many students say it helps to talk with other students about logic. There is something about logic discussions that can expand our mind and answer questions. But a group setting is not required.

Each lesson ends with exercises. Each exercise builds on previous exercises, so don't wait until the end of the lesson to check your answers. Check as you go. This way, you will know if you are misunderstanding something.

If you don't understand something in a lesson, do the exercises anyway. We designed them to be teaching tools. You may catch something in the exercises that you didn't understand while reading. If you still don't understand, repeat the lesson. You can also discuss your difficulties with someone else.

This book is a springboard to larger projects. For students, larger projects may include a science fair experiment, a history research paper, or starting a small business selling snails. Adults may wish to use the thinking tools in this book to solve problems like motivating their children to sell lemonade instead of snails. Whatever you do, don't simply read this book and then forget about these tools.

In a Classroom

If you visit our Web site, www.christianlogic.com, you will find a forum where teachers share suggestions on how to use our books in a classroom. Teachers could have students work on the larger projects mentioned at the end of this book or play one of the logic games.

The Challenge

We thought we would close with an inspiring challenge to battle the forces of bad reasoning. But instead, we will suggest you read the next lesson.

Tools for Thinking

Lesson 1

A Thinking Tool

Consider the following situation. Let's say your mom sent you to the drugstore to buy a bottle of aspirin. While you are walking home, a black van pulls up next to you. A guy with a beard leans out of the window . . .

BEARDED GUY: Hey, kid, you want a bag of candy? Here, get in the van quick and I'll take you for a ride. Don't worry. Your mom said it was okay.

YOU: Just a moment, let me think about it. How do I know you are telling the truth?

At this moment, you need to know whether you can trust the bearded man in the black van. Is he telling you the truth? Did your mom really say it was okay to go with him? You need some tools.

This book is like a toolbox. This book is full of different kinds of tools you can use for different thinking tasks. Just as you take a wrench out of a regular toolbox and use it to fix the sink, so you can use the tools we give you in this book to solve thinking problems.

A thinking tool will often take the form of a question. "How do I know this person is trustworthy? Does he have a reason to lie? Are there two sides to this story? Which one should I believe?" Thinking tools are very useful in solving many kinds of problems – from studying history, to finding out why the family cow is sick, to knowing whether to trust bearded guys in black vans.

> BEARDED GUY: C'mon, kid, do you think I'd lie to you?
>
> YOU: Are you a primary source?
>
> GUY: Huh?
>
> YOU: I mean, did you see the events in question yourself, or hear them from others? What about biases? Do you have a reason to lie?
>
> GUY: Umm.
>
> YOU: And other evidence – do you have any corroborating evidence for what you say? Perhaps other witnesses, or some circumstantial evidence?
>
> GUY: Who?
>
> YOU: So you admit that all you have is hearsay evidence and possibility reasoning? My daddy said I was not supposed to talk to strangers.

Each lesson in this book will give you a thinking tool or will teach you how to use a tool. By the time you finish this book, you will have many tools in your thinking toolbox – tools such as:

- How to list reasons to believe something
- How to analyze opposing viewpoints
- Examining evidence and sources
- Brainstorming
- The scientific method

However, the tool we should learn in this lesson is probably one which I am sure your mother and your father have already taught you.

Just because somebody tells you something, that doesn't mean it is true.

Unless that somebody is somebody you know very well.

YOU: Wait a second . . . I guess I'll get in the car. Where do you want to go?

BEARDED GUY: What?! No, you don't want to get in here. You aren't supposed to trust strangers. Your father told you many times not to trust strangers!

YOU: That's right, but I think it's okay to trust this one, Dad.

BEARDED GUY: What?! Oh. What gave me away?

YOU: It was the beard. It's the same one you used in the Christmas play.

DAD: Did I fool you for a little while?

YOU: No, but it sure gave me a chance to try out those tools I've been learning in *The Thinking Toolbox*.

DAD: I'd say you deserve some ice cream for cracking this case.

YOU: Sounds good!

Exercises

A. For each of the following quotes, say whether you would trust what the person is saying.

1. LIBRARIAN: It says here in the *Australian Guide to Poisonous Snakes* that the Australian death adder is easily recognized by its triangular-shaped head, short stout body, and thin tail. It says death adders have a toxic venom. Before the introduction of antivenin, about 60% of bites to humans were fatal. It says that if you are bitten by a death adder, you should seek medical attention immediately.

2. MAN NEXT TO YOU ON PLANE: I read somewhere in a book that the Australian death adder isn't really as dangerous as they make it out to be. I read that if you ever get bit by one, all you have to do is drink a quart of lemon juice – the acid will kill the venom. It's true because I read it in a book written by somebody who was an authority on how to treat poisonous snake bites.

3. AUSTRALIAN BUSHMAN: Aye, that's a nasty snake, mate. They call it the Australian death adder. I wouldn't touch it if I were you – very poisonous. I was bit by one once – they nearly 'ad to take my leg off at the knee.

4. YOUR MORTAL ENEMY: Ah, don't believe him. That isn't an Australian death adder; it's just an Eastern tiger snake. They're perfectly harmless. I would know – I'm an expert on Australian snakes. You can pick it up if you like.

5. *Australian Guide to Poisonous Snakes*: The Eastern tiger snake inhabits the southern portion of Africa. The venom of an Eastern tiger snake is of no consequence to humans, but they will strike readily when provoked.

B. 6. Which of the following persons does not agree with the other two?

FRED: I think we're lost. I think we're going in circles. We have been traveling in this Brazilian jungle for a week, and I keep seeing the same scenery.

DERF: We're not lost. The jungle looks the same no matter where you go. Besides, we've been floating downstream on this river. Rivers don't go in circles. If we just keep floating, we'll end up in Cairo, just like this guidebook I bought says.

ENROD: I don't know about that. I've been looking at this guidebook, and it says

Cairo is in Egypt. Besides, all the signs I've seen have been printed in Arabic. I don't think we're in the Brazilian jungle anymore. I think we're lost.

C. 7. Which of the following do you think presents the most convincing argument?

a. "I think hiking in the Rocky Mountains is much more enjoyable than hiking in the Appalachian Mountains because the Rocky Mountains are much taller, which makes the scenery better and more varied. Also, the Rocky Mountains are filled with pine forests, which means there is less underbrush to walk through when you hike. Also, due to the drier climate out west, there are fewer bugs to bother you."

b. "I think hiking in the Appalachian Mountains is more enjoyable than hiking in the Rocky Mountains because the Appalachians aren't as tall. This makes it much easier to hike, which means you won't get as tired and you will be able to enjoy the scenery better. Also, I find deciduous forests are much more beautiful than pine forests, especially in the fall. Also, because it's more humid, your skin won't dry out."

D. 8. Read the following story and decide what happened.

> *Sheriff Handy was no pilgrim. He had been over the trail more than once and had seen both ends of a six-gun before he settled in the town of Chimneysmoke.*
>
> *So when Sheriff Handy saw the stranger ride into town, he knew trouble was just around the corner. And that's where the stranger went, around the corner into the Cockroach Café.*
>
> *The sheriff pulled a wanted poster off his office wall and strode in the direction of the Cockroach Café. He thought he knew the stranger, and he was going to find out. Halfway across the street, the sheriff heard shots coming out of the Café.*
>
> SHERIFF HANDY: Looks like the trouble's already started.
>
> *Sheriff Handy pushed the swinging doors open and surveyed the scene in the Cockroach Café. The stranger stood in the middle of the room. On each side of him was a man, lying on the floor, shot dead, his six-shooter still in his hand. There was a smell of gunsmoke, but the stranger had no gun.*
>
> SHERIFF HANDY: Who saw what happened here?
>
> WANDA WAITRESS: I saw something, sheriff. I saw that stranger come in the door there, then sit down between those two gents – the ones who are dead now. Then I sees both those gents notice that stranger, then they go for their guns, and start shooting at the stranger. There was a lot of noise and gunsmoke, then I sees

both those two men dead on the floor.

SIDEWINDER SAM: I didn't see what happened, but I'm pretty sure I heard only two guns go off, then I looks and sees those two men on the floor. That stranger must be mighty quick with a gun – those two men were mean hombres. That one's name was Pokerface Pete and the other they just called The Kid. They used to be in the Deadeye Gang along with Deadeye Dan, until the gang kicked them out. They swore they'd get even with Deadeye Dan, though.

Sheriff Handy noticed that one bullet was gone from each of the dead men's guns. Sheriff Handy walked up to the stranger.

SHERIFF HANDY: Are you the notorious criminal Deadeye Dan?

STRANGER: No, you must be mistaken. My name's Rusty. People keep mistakin' me for Deadeye Dan, but I've never seen him before. I ain't done nuthin. See, I don't even have a gun! I just came in here to get a bite to eat.

Lesson 2

A Discussion, a Disagreement, an Argument, and a Fight

Most conversations can be put into one of four categories – a discussion, a disagreement, an argument, or a fight. Let's look at what we mean.

> KATHY: Hello, Roberta. How have things been going?
>
> ROBERTA: Fine, but I wish it would rain. My petunias are nearly dried up. There isn't supposed to be any rain today.
>
> KATHY: The extended forecast said we'd have rain later this week.

This conversation is only a discussion. Kathy and Roberta are sharing information. They both might not have the same information, but they agree with one another.

A discussion

Here is a disagreement:

ROBERTA: Oh, I hope so. Where did you hear it was going to rain?
KATHY: It was on The Weather Channel. I always watch The Weather Channel for my weather.
ROBERTA: Really? I prefer Accuweather.com.

Now Roberta has a difference of opinion with Kathy. Roberta likes Accuweather.com better than The Weather Channel. They are still having a discussion, but now they disagree. However, neither feels that she needs to convince the other. Let's see what happens when they try to convince one another.

A disagreement

KATHY: I think The Weather Channel is more accurate. It seems like every time they predict a storm, it happens. I wouldn't go to Accuweather.com if I were you. They don't seem to be as accurate.
ROBERTA: Not in my experience. I'm sure The Weather Channel is a good source for weather news, but nothing beats Accuweather.com for accuracy. Accuweather.com received the "Windy" award from the National Meteorologists Association for being the most accurate weather source.

Now Roberta and Kathy are giving evidence for what they think. They are having an argument.

An argument

I know that sounds like a nasty word – argument – but it isn't bad. It just means that Kathy and Roberta think it is appropriate to use evidence and reasoning to convince one another. As long as they talk civilly, there isn't a problem.

Someone is presenting an argument *anytime he states a viewpoint and gives reasons to support it. Anytime two or more people are engaged in stating differing views and reasons for these views, they are* having an argument.

What gives the word "argument" a bad name is when it turns into something else – a fight.

KATHY: Oh, really. I'll bet you made that up. I'll bet there's no National Meteorologists Association.

ROBERTA: I didn't make it up. What are you insinuating?

KATHY: You're always making things up to sound smart. If you ask me, you haven't said a true word for years.

ROBERTA: At least I'm not a little-hen-clucking-gossip like you. I'll take my hat and leave.

KATHY: I hope your petunias shrivel up and get eaten by a striped cucumber beetle.

Kathy and Roberta are fighting now. This type of conversation is never appropriate. Kathy and Roberta aren't talking about where to go for a weather forecast anymore; they are attacking and insulting each other. Kathy is calling Roberta a liar, and Roberta is calling Kathy a gossip – both nasty names. There is no clear line where an argument becomes a fight, but anytime both people become strongly emotionally involved or start insulting each other, it is probably a fight.

A fight

1. **People are having a discussion anytime they exchange ideas.**

2. **A disagreement is an exchange of differing views.**

3. **An argument is an exchange of differing views as well as reasons for these views.**

4. **A fight is an exchange of attacks and insults.**

Exercises

Identify each of the following examples as a discussion, a disagreement, an argument, or a fight.

1. MOM: Joey, it's time for you to go to bed.
   JOEY: I don't want to go to bed. I want to stay up.

2. FRED: Ouch. That bee stung me.
   DERF: That wasn't a bee; it was a wasp. You can tell because bees can fly. That wasp just slithered along the ground.
   FRED: No, it has to be a bee. It made a rattling noise. Wasps don't rattle before they sting, silly.
   DERF: I still think it's a wasp. Bees sting with their tails, and that wasp bit you.

3. SUZY: Let's go play house.
   KABEL: I'd rather play store.

4. MR.: Honey, I bought you flowers for your birthday.
   MRS.: Today isn't my birthday; that was last month.
   MR.: I mean our anniversary.
   MRS.: That's next month.
   MR.: Sorry, honey, I forgot.
   MRS.: That's okay. Thanks for the flowers.

5. TOM: Where should we go out to eat?
   SUSAN: I like Steak and Shake; let's go there
   TOM: Okay.

6. MAN WITH BIG HAT: Good morning ma'am. I come from the county sheriff's office, and I'm afraid we've had a report that you were threatening some salesmen with a shotgun. Is this true?
   MRS. OAKLEY: It weren't no shotgun. I was usin' my express rifle, .700 Nitro Magnum.

7. MR.: See, Honey, I bought you flowers for our anniversary. They're blue, just like on our wedding day.
   MRS.: No, those were red.
   MR.: Blue.

8. MR.: See, Honey, I bought you flowers for your birthday.

MRS.: Yeah right, you're just trying to be nice so I won't be mad at you for mowing over my delphiniums. You don't care about me.

MR.: If you just wouldn't plant your ridiculous flowers at odd places, perhaps I could remember where not to mow.

MRS.: Don't give me that; you know I told you not to mow there.

MR.: No you didn't. All you said was don't mow over the delwhatchamacallthems. How am I supposed to know what they look like?

Lesson 3

When It Is Dumb to Argue

While it is nearly always okay to have a discussion with someone, sometimes it is not appropriate to disagree, and sometimes it is not appropriate to have an argument. It is rarely appropriate to fight.

For example, if the Queen of England walked up and introduced herself, it would be appropriate to have a pleasant discussion with her. However, it probably would not be proper to disagree with her – at least not at that moment. And it certainly wouldn't be appropriate to argue or fight.

But let's say you were a student in a classroom and the teacher said something very wrong. Let's say he said the king cobra of southeast Asia is not poisonous, but is really a cuddly snake who likes to be kissed on the nose. In this situation, it would be okay to stand up and disagree. And depending on the type of class you were in, it might be okay to argue with him – explaining that the king cobra is poisonous, how it injects a powerful neurotoxic venom, and how without prompt medical aid, death is certain for its victims.

Sometimes it is a waste of time to argue.

FRED: What is the capital of South Dakota? I have no idea.

DERF: I don't know. Maybe it's Tulsa?

FRED: I think it's Los Angeles. That sounds Swedish, and I know there are lots of Swedish people in South Dakota.

DERF: No way. It's got to be Tulsa. My grandmother was Swedish, and she said she once visited Tulsa.

Both Fred and Derf admitted they didn't know what the capital of South Dakota was, but they are arguing about it anyway. Until one of them looks it up in an atlas, they are wasting their time.

There are other times when we shouldn't argue.

GUY: Hey, you! I think you parked just a little too close to my car – move it.

HANS: Actually, I was in this parking spot before you came. You were the one who parked close to me.

GUY: Don't be a smart-alec to me, Bub. Just move your car over.

Sometimes arguing can be dangerous. This man is obviously upset and isn't thinking clearly, so arguing about who was in the parking space first would probably only make him more angry.

"Do not answer a fool according to his folly, lest you also be like him" (Proverbs 26:4 NKJV).

When might it be dumb to argue?

1. **When it wouldn't be socially appropriate at the time.**

2. **When neither person has any real knowledge about the subject being argued.**

3. **When one of the persons involved is angry or isn't thinking clearly.**

Exercises

A. In the following situations, do you think it would be appropriate to argue?

1. ATHEIST: There is no God, and I can prove it. If God created the earth, why is there so much death and destruction in the world? Either God doesn't exist or He doesn't care about us.
   YOU: I beg to differ with that.

2. HANS: Good grief, this article is 1,400 words long and it is supposed to

be only 700. I'll need to cut out a lot.
NATHANIEL: Actually, I remember we were allowed 723 words.
HANS: No. I distinctly remember 700.
NATHANIEL: 723.

3. JUDGE: According to my information, you have been charged with jay-walking on a public street. How do you plead?
    PLAINTIFF: Not guilty, your honor.

4. CALLER: I can't believe you think it is okay to use the term "niggardly" on the radio. You're a racist.
    TALK SHOW GUEST: Actually, the term "niggardly" has nothing to do with race at all. It simply means to be covetous and miserly. You can look it up in the dictionary.
    CALLER: Yeah, right. It's obvious you're a racist.

5. AUSTIN: I got you. I shot you with my ray gun. You're dead now.
    ADAM: But I have atomic armor on. It reflects your ray gun back at you, so you're dead and I'm not.
    AUSTIN: But my ray gun is armor-piercing. You're dead.
    ADAM: But my armor has a special layer that stops armor-piercing rays.
    AUSTIN: My ray gun is special. It goes though that layer.

6. A blond Australian guy hands Queen Elizabeth an Australian death adder: 'Ere she is. Isn't she a beaut? Aye. Don't be scared. She's perfectly harmless; she would never bite a queen.

B. In the following examples, is the speaker presenting an argument?

7. "I believe there is a God because if there wasn't a God there would be no purpose to life."

8. PAUL: What shall we say then? Is there unrighteousness with God? Certainly not! For He says to Moses, "I will have mercy on whomever I will have mercy, and I will have compassion on whomever I will have compassion."

9. MRS. OAKLEY: Howdy.

10. JESUS: Lazarus, come forth!

11. "And God said to Noah . . . 'Make yourself an ark of gopherwood: make

rooms in the ark, and cover it inside and outside with pitch.'" – Genesis 6:14

12. "You dirty rotten bum, why did you cut me off in traffic like that?"

13. "Studying logical thinking skills isn't only about learning how to come up with mind-bogglingly good arguments to defeat an opponent's argument and 'show him what's right.' Learning when it is appropriate to argue is also very important."

14. "Okay, this gun here's loaded, so everybody start emptying your pockets and purses – and don't forget the jewelry."

Lesson 4

Fact, Inference, or Opinion

Sometimes people will say things which are ambiguous – that is, we can't be sure what they mean.

> NEWSPAPER ARTICLE: Homeschooling should be banned. These homeschoolers are not teaching their kids the things they need to learn. Fifty percent of homeschooled kids can't read properly, and 75% of homeschooled kids aren't getting enough socialization. In fact, there are some homeschooled kids who are actually being abused by their parents.

While there is nothing ambiguous about what this reporter thinks about homeschooling, there are parts of this statement which we are not sure how to take. For example, how does he *know* that 50 percent of homeschooled kids can't read? Did he find a study which said this? Or is it just his own guess? Does he *know* some homeschooled kids who have been abused, or is this just what he *thinks*? He asserts these things as if they were facts, but they may only be his opinions.

When we make a statement, we are either stating (1) what we think is a fact, (2) what we have inferred from facts, or (3) opinion. We often do not clearly state which of these three categories we are speaking in.

Fact

PROSECUTING ATTORNEY: Mr. Jones, what did you see on the night in question?

MR. JONES: Well, it was like this. I was sitting on my porch and saw that man right there sneak up to Mr. Applebottom's house, break the window, and crawl inside. He had a gun, so I called the cops.

We can call Mr. Jones's testimony a *statement of fact*. Mr. Jones is describing things which he saw happen – things which other witnesses might verify if they were there.

A statement of fact *is any statement about something which can be directly observed by others or checked for accuracy.*

Something is a statement of fact if we can check to see if it is true. This does not mean the statement is necessarily true. The witness might be lying, but at least we can check up on him and find out for sure.

Inference

PROSECUTING ATTORNEY: Sheriff, what happened when you got there?

SHERIFF: When I entered the house, I saw Mr. Applebottom on the floor, shot dead, and the defendant standing there with a smoking gun in his hand. I didn't see anybody else in the house, so I figured that man must have been the killer. So I arrested him.

This sheriff saw some evidence in front of him, and he drew a logical inference from those facts. He is making a *statement of inference* from the facts he sees.

A statement of inference *is a logical conclusion made from verifiable facts.*

This sheriff's inference is probably true, but it might not be. First, his inference might not be logically drawn from his facts. If the sheriff were to take the facts that he sees and conclude that the man with the gun must be the Loch Ness Monster, he wouldn't be making a logical inference.

Also, the sheriff might not have had all the evidence he needed to make a good inference. There might have been somebody else he didn't see, hiding in the house, who really committed the crime. The man standing there with the gun might have picked it up after the real murderer fled.

Opinion

PROSECUTING ATTORNEY: Can you tell us . . .

MISS PINK: Oh, yes I can. I looked out the window and saw the sheriff bringing that man right there out of poor Mr. Applebottom's house. I didn't like the look of the man, and I said to my sister, "That man just murdered somebody."

Miss Pink is expressing a *statement of opinion*. She is taking facts and adding other information to them which cannot be directly observed or checked for accuracy. This is her opinion of what she thinks the man is like.

A statement of opinion *is a statement of inference that is not entirely backed with verifiable facts.*

While part of Miss Pink's opinion is based on facts, a good part of what she thinks is not based on any facts. It is based on what she feels about the man. She might be right, but it's just her opinion. Because an opinion is often based on feelings, it is even less reliable than a fact or an inference.

So, How Do We Tell Which is Which?

It is often difficult to determine whether something is a fact, an inference, or just an opinion. Authors commonly interweave fact, inference, and opinion into their writing without telling us which is which. Often people say things as if they were facts or inferences when they are really just their opinions.

LETTER TO EDITOR: Yeah, and I think 79.8876% of homeschoolers aren't very smart.

Since facts must be able to be checked for accuracy, this last statement is not a fact. How could we check to verify if 79.8876% of homeschoolers aren't very smart? "Smart" is not a well-defined term. We could not check to verify what he is saying.

When someone will not explain what facts he used to come to his conclusion, he is often just giving his opinion.

Exercises

A. Are the following examples statements of fact, statements of inference, or statements of opinion?

1. "The book *Moby-Dick* is a novel about a whale. It is a long novel, longer than *A Christmas Carol*."

2. BOB: Howdy, what's your name?
   ISHMAEL: Call me Ishmael.
   BOB: You mean your name is Ishmael?

3. "*Moby-Dick* is the most boring novel in existence!"

4. "*Moby-Dick* is a dramatic story with movement and suspense and human passion."

5. "I've read *Moby-Dick,* and just about half of the novel is the author describing the habits and abilities of whales, as well as the methods for killing them. The author of *Moby-Dick* must have known a lot about whales."

6. "*Moby-Dick* is the high-water mark of Herman Melville's achievements. Its narrative and record of fact are superior to those of his earlier works, *Typee* and *Omoo*."

7. "Whales are true air-breathing, warm-blooded, viviparous mammals. The act of spouting or blowing is the exhalation of the air from the lungs." – *Webster's Dictionary*

8. "Seventy-five percent of Herman Melville's novels are boring."

9. "Many think of whales as big fish, but whales are mammals, just as we are. Millions of years ago the ancestors of whales lived on land. It is hard to imagine, but these early creatures had nostrils, hair, and legs."

10. "The Bible says that murdering a human being is wrong. The Bible also says that purposely killing a baby before it is born is murder. So, the Bible must say abortion is wrong."

11. FRED: I want to be homeschooled. Seventy-six percent of homeschoolers have a higher IQ than kids who go to public school.
DERF: How do you know that?
FRED: It's just true.

12. "The Talons are the most skilled baseball team this year. They have the best players and the best organization. I'm pretty sure they will win the World Series this year."

13. "*The Lord of the Rings* is the longest movie series ever made in New Zealand."

14. "Robberies in this town are at the highest levels they have ever been."

15. OFFICER: Can you tell me what happened, ma'am?
MA'AM: Yes, sir, I can. I was standing right here on this curb when that man purposely slammed his truck into the back end of that car. I couldn't believe he did it on purpose.

16. "Crime in this town is at the highest levels it has ever been. In fact, it's rising all over the country. We need to do something about this skyrocketing crime, or soon we will be held hostage in our homes by thugs."

B. Are the following inferences warranted?

17. SHERIFF: I walked into the saloon and saw that man over there with a smoking gun in his hand. Then I looked over on the other side of the room and there was a dead man on the floor. He had a smoking gun in his hand too. I figured it was a case of self-defense, so I didn't arrest nobody.

18. SHERIFF: I walked into the saloon and saw that man over there with a smoking gun in his hand. Then I looked over on the other side of the room and there was a dead man with a hole clean through him. I figured that the dead man must have been gored by a bull elephant, so I went off to trail the elephant. I didn't arrest nobody because I never found the elephant.

19. SHERIFF: I walked into the saloon and saw that man over there with a smoking gun in his hand. Then I looked over on the other side of the room and there was a dead man with a bullet hole clean through him. I figured somebody in the saloon must have seen what happened, so I asked the bartender what happened.

20. SCAR FACE: It was self-defense, sheriff. I was busy robbing the bank when the teller said, "You won't get away with this." I figured he was gonna kill me, so I shot him.

C. 21. Which person in the following conversation is stating a fact, which person is stating an inference, and which person which is stating an opinion?

a. FELICE: Every book in this library has a magnetic strip on it so that the book cannot leave the building without sounding the alarm. However, if a book has been checked out, it won't sound the alarm if it leaves the building.

b. HEWEY: That's true! That would mean that if a book is missing and the alarm bell hasn't sounded, then the missing book has either been checked out without us noticing, or it is still in the library.

c. LAMONT: I think the missing book is miles away from here by now. The thief has probably sold it on eBay.

Lesson 5

Finding the Premises and Conclusion

An argument *is a statement that uses premises and a conclusion and that usually tries to convince you of something.*

> BINGO'S MOTHER: Bingo, I really wish you'd leave your shoes on while we're in the car. Nobody likes the smell, and we might have to get out of the car and you'll need them on.
> BINGO: Okay.

Notice that Bingo's mother used a simple argument to convince him to put his shoes back on. Her argument contained two parts:

1. Premises – (1) Nobody likes the smell, and (2) we might have to get out of the car and you'll need them on.
2. Conclusion – I really wish you'd leave your shoes on. . . .

The *conclusion* is what Bingo's mother wanted to convince him was true. And the *premises* are the evidence or reasons she used to convince him. Arguments are often more complicated than this, but if we remember these two basic parts, our job will be much easier.

Finding the premises and conclusion in an argument is the first step towards understanding the argument. Sometimes a conclusion will appear at the beginning of an argument, sometimes at the end, and on rare occasions, you'll be shocked to discover it in the middle. Premises are even harder to find.

> WARNING MESSAGE: Do your best to conserve wood products. Deforestation may be causing our earth to spin faster. In the same way that a figure skater's

rate of spin increases when she brings her arms close to her body, if we cut down tall trees, this may cause our planet to spin dangerously fast. Together we can save our planet.

This is a simple argument. The conclusion probably is the combination of the first and last sentences, "Save our planet by conserving wood products." The single premise is something like "Tall trees act like the arms of a figure skater and if we cut them down, our planet will spin out of control."

PROFESSOR OF ETYMOLOGY AT OXBRIDGE: "When in Rome, do as the Romans do." This is a very important principle to remember. I always open my classes with this phrase. The reasons are manifold and multiplicitous. To quote our learned sage, "To be or not to be, that is the question." And truly, it is. For how could we perambulate the penumbral cabinet that is our lives without phrases like, "When in Rome, do as the Romans do"? Why, life would be a total bore. We can question all the verbosity of learned sayings, but without "When in Rome, do as the Romans do," we are left standing in the gutter of human intellect. A classical education is but the vaunted vantage point for a vociferous – dare I say venomous or vicarious – vocation. Even the much-maligned poet Horatio Haldeger was fond of saying . . .

Relax. Paragraphs like this usually don't have any point. If they do, here are some hints to help you find it.

1. **First, find the conclusion. Ask: what is the author's point? Words like "therefore" and "so" are clues that a conclusion may follow.**

2. **Find one or two premises. Ask: does this author use any facts or reasoning to persuade us?**

3. **Underline key sentences or put numbers in the margin to mark premises.**

A good author will make this work easy for you.

In the paragraph above by the Professor of Etymology, the conclusion probably is "Life would be a total bore without phrases like 'When in Rome, do as the Romans do.'" One premise may be "Without 'When in Rome, do as the Romans do,' we are left standing in the gutter of human intellect." Another premise, hidden in the quote "To be or not to be, that is the question," might be expanded as "If we don't have phrases like this, then there is no reason to live." But this last premise is hard to ferret out.

This paragraph was a bit thick. We want to show you how difficult it can be to find conclusions and premises. If you can handle this, you can understand any argument.

Exercises

In the following examples, decide whether the author intended this to be an argument. If it is an argument, find the conclusion and at least one premise.

1. "But Mom! I might die before dinner, and I'm going out to play in the weeds, and I might forget to eat it later, and Grandma gave it to me to have when I wanted, and I feel sick and maybe I'll have a stomachache

and won't be able to eat it, and I want my candy now!"

2. "This book is green and that honey is sweet. The Cubs will win next season."

3. "I believe the earth is flat. Ever since I was a little child, my mother taught me to pray for my father that he wouldn't fall off the edge of the earth when he left in his whaleboat. And we all can see when we look around us that the earth is flat. If it were curved, every time I set a ball on the ground, it would roll off downhill. How absurd."

4. "The cheetah is the fastest-running land animal.
My Jeep was fast when it had gas.
This rope is tied fast to this cheetah.
I am holding the other end."

5. "It's warm outside and I think the bugs might start coming out. I hate bugs, but last year there weren't as many. Isn't it interesting how each year is different? I'm glad we have bugs. It'd be horrible if God made rocks that could crawl and you'd find them in your soup and things. Which reminds me, I need to plant my spinach. I'll need it to make spinach soup. So I need someone to change the oil in the car because I'm going into town."

6. WIFE: Dear, do you love me?
HUSBAND: Of course.
WIFE: Then why don't you buy me more flowers?
HUSBAND: I didn't know you wanted any.
WIFE: See, you don't love me. Every woman loves flowers, and if you loved me you'd give me flowers.

7. PROMOTIONAL PAMPHLET: Midwestern towns are choice places to visit. No one uses security systems around here, or even locks doors. You never meet strangers – you know everyone, even the sheriff!

8. "The earth is round we all know, for fishes flat do not grow.
If in winter round we flew,
the snow would blow off and not stick like glue.
When I with mittens stare in cold, at a glistening white remold,
I should see . . ."
   – Ingrid Lifferman, 1703.

9. In *Right Ho, Jeeves* by P. G. Wodehouse, Bertie Wooster describes Miss Madeline Bassett as follows: "Her conversation, to my mind, was of a nature calculated to excite the liveliest suspicions. Well, I mean to say, when a girl suddenly asks you out of a blue sky if you don't sometimes feel that the stars are God's daisy chain, you begin to think a bit."

10. "Philosophy is all a bunch of bunk. Philosophers just like to talk a lot about stupid stuff. You can't prove a thing they say . . . it's all in their heads. If there's a war, we should send all the philosophy professors to the front lines. They'd probably like it out there watching the bullets go whizzing by and asking each other if the bullets really exist."

11. "My sisters don't like the road commissioner. He cut down the trees to build a new bridge at the creek. My sisters think the old bridge was fine. The hole in the middle made people slow down when they pass our house. Besides, he could build a new bridge around the trees. And the trees are older than the road commissioner is, so they should have a say. My sisters think the commissioner wouldn't stop his bulldozer even if there were an old lady standing in front of it."

12. FAMOUS ACTOR: Tonight we will bring you a new form of entertainment. You will watch me eat twenty-five live snails in an attempt to keep you from turning the channel to a different station.

13. In an advertisement a famous actress walks on stage, "I've lost seventy-three pounds. You can too." The scene shifts to a chef preparing food. The famous actress says, "You can prepare non-nutritive foods your family can't resist. Just add our advanced Slendra formula. You'll eat knowing you won't gain a single ounce." An animated scene appears showing food molecules being coated by Slendra formula, making them indigestible.

14. "When a cat falls, it always lands on its feet. And when a piece of toast is dropped, it always lands with the jelly side down. Scientists have proposed that we strap large slabs of jellied toast to the backs of large cats. The two opposing forces (toast and cats) would cause each cat-toast combination to hover, spinning inches above the ground. We could build a high-speed electric train that would float on thousands of these cat-toast devices."

Lesson 6

How to List Reasons Why You Believe Something

Daniel was eighteen years old, and it was time he decided if he wanted to be Amish. Amish families allow their children to make this decision.

Daniel's family lived near several "English" farms. ("English" means they are not Amish.) Daniel's English friends knew he struggled with this question, and they prodded him to explain why electricity and cars were sinful. He felt frustrated because he'd already told them these things aren't sinful; Amish have simply chosen not to live with them. But Daniel wasn't able to explain why – or at least not clearly.

Daniel felt that if he couldn't explain Amish convictions, he probably would not have the strength to practice them all his life.

Reasons Why You Believe

We may not understand why the Amish live without electricity and cars, but we can respect their beliefs. We all have beliefs. We believe that murder is wrong. We believe we know what our name is. We believe that when we drop this book, it will fall on the floor and not fly up and hover around the ceiling.

However, many of us do not understand why we believe what we believe. Or we may think we understand, but we have difficulty explaining it to others.

To understand a belief, we need to understand the reasons that point to it. We keep track of our reasons in our heads, even though we may not be aware we're doing this.

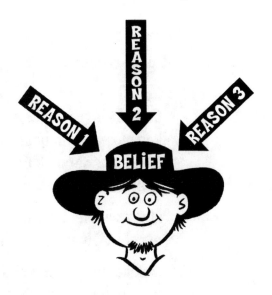

If someone asked Daniel why he doesn't own a car, what would he say? He can't say, "I believe I shouldn't own a car because I believe I shouldn't own a car." He needs to list his reasons.

List Your Reasons

Juddrey and Bubba are trying to get Daniel to buy a truck.

BUBBA: Man, if you got a truck, you'd really be cool. And you could go into town whenever you want and see a movie or something. You live the most totally boring life. I couldn't stand it.

Many people don't think about their reasons. Their thought life may never go deeper than this.

List your reasons:

1. **Recall the history of how you came to your belief. List key moments in your life when you began thinking in a certain direction.**

2. **What people, books, or events influenced you?**

3. **Talk to people who share your beliefs and ask them for their reasons.**

Be willing to acknowledge reasons that don't sound good. Did you adopt a belief because everyone told you to believe it? Be honest with yourself. Don't be embarrassed to think about these things. If you are sincere in this, God will help you find an answer.

DANIEL: We don't use cars because this helps us live a quiet life. We're not tempted to have status symbols. People out there complain their life is too busy, but we've never had this problem. We value our community most of all and how it supports a godly lifestyle. This is the life we enjoy. But I admit a truck sure would come in handy.

We may not agree with Daniel, but we can respect his effort to explain his reasons to us.

Sort Your Reasons

JENNY: I believe eating fruit for breakfast is good for me.

BERT: Why?

JENNY: Fruit is the most natural food, and I feel better when I eat it. Plus, it has lots of antioxidants and vitamins. And I've read vegetarians live longer.

BERT: But you're not a vegetarian.

JENNY: Well, the more fruit I eat, the more vitamins I get.

BERT: But you can take vitamin pills for that.

JENNY: I know, but they're not the natural vitamins I get in fruit.

BERT: This plastic cup is 100 percent natural. God made every atom in it like he made every atom in a vitamin C pill.

JENNY: When it comes down to it, I just feel better when I eat fruit. It gives me energy all morning, and I feel nice and hungry when lunch comes around.

BERT: I can't argue with that.

Jenny explained her reasons for eating fruit for breakfast. Bert helped her prioritize her reasons until she found the most important one. We can sort our reasons by putting ones we feel confident about in one column and reasons we are not confident about in another column.

Conclusion

NORMA: I can't believe you're eating those!

LUCY: They're good! Crunchy with gooey, sweet stuff inside. I love the chocolate star-shaped ones. Mmmmm.

NORMA: Read what it says on the box! They're chocolate-covered bugs!

LUCY: Ahaaaa! Where on earth did these come from! If that little brother of mine . . .

NORMA: No. I was wrong. It says they're imitation chocolate-covered bugs. See, the ingredients say they're made of puffed corn.

LUCY: Wheeew. I was starting to feel sick. . . . Wait a minute. It says puffed corn, but the next ingredient says 100 percent organic arthropods and arachnids. What does that mean?

What we believe affects what we do. If we believe we're eating candy, we feel fine. If we believe we're eating bugs, we stop. This is why it is important to understand why we believe what we believe. You can use the tools in the next lessons to strengthen your reasons.

Exercises

A. Find the beliefs stated in the following examples. If you can think of some beliefs that are implied, but aren't stated, list these also.

1. NATHANIEL: I believe I'm a better foosball player.
   HANS: How's this?
   NATHANIEL: I move my players faster than you, I shoot the ball quicker, and the foosball table gets jerked in my direction because I'm using more energy.
   HANS: I think I'm better because I win more games.

2. NORMA: You're hurting my feelings. Why did you talk to me that way?
   LUCY: I can say what I want after what you did.
   NORMA: What did I do? If I knew, I could apologize.
   Lucy: You told Jacob that my beekeeping business was a sticky mess. I work hard with my bees, and I believe I've sold more honey bottles this year than ever. I can't believe you said it was a sticky mess.

Norma: I'm sorry. I meant that your honey was sticky, not that your business was a failure.

B. List some reasons why someone might believe the following things are true. List both good and bad reasons. Answers may vary.

3. "The earth is a sphere and not flat like a pancake."

4. "The earth is flat like a pancake and not a sphere."

5. "Mint chocolate chip ice cream tastes good."

6. "Ford makes better trucks than Chevy."

7. "Your bedroom door is a portal into an alien world."

C. The following are some common beliefs. After each belief is a list of possible reasons someone might have for that belief. Indicate whether you think these reasons are good or bad. Answers may vary.

8. BELIEF: Murder is wrong.

   REASONS:

   a. Murder kills someone.

   b. The Bible says murder is wrong.

   c. Because the word "murder" begins with the letter "m," and I know a guy named Murdock who's really mean and I don't like him because his name starts with the letter "m."

   d. For thousands of years of history every culture has condemned murder.

   e. The cops will come and put you in jail if you kill someone.

   f. If we allowed murder in our nation, then it would be hard to live a happy and productive life.

9. BELIEF: The earth is shaped like a sphere and not flat like a pancake.

   REASONS:

   a. My parents told me. Everybody I know believes it. All the books I've read say it.

b. I've seen pictures from outer space.

c. The horizon looks flat, but this is only because we can't see over the curvature of the earth.

d. If the earth were flat, then the rivers would not be able to flow anywhere.

e. In Illinois, where it is flat, you can see only the tops of the grain silos many miles away.

10. BELIEF: Honeybees do not sting when foraging for nectar. They only sting when protecting their hives.

REASONS:

a. I'm a beginner beekeeper, and I know this is true.

b. Mr. A. I. Root told me this, and he's been keeping bees for a long time.

c. I read this in my beekeeping manual.

d. I read this in an article by a famous movie actress who was selling a beauty lotion that contains bee-sting venom for removing wrinkles from your face.

Lesson 7

How to Defeat Your Own Argument

After you have listed all the reasons why you believe something, the next step is to defeat the argument you have built. This may sound like a strange thing to do, but if you don't try to defeat your own argument, someone else will.

BINGO: I believe that the earth was created by God in six days. That's what God says in the Bible.

PROFESSOR: So you believe the book of Genesis is true? But what about the contradictions in it? Genesis says plants were created on the third day, but the sun wasn't created until the fourth day – how did the plants exist without any light? Also, how did Noah fit all the animals on the ark? And where did Cain get his wife?

BINGO: Err, uhm, anyway, I believe that the earth is only six thousand years old, because if there were a sun millions of years ago, it would have been so large nobody could have lived on the earth.

PROFESSOR: Do you? What about dating methods? Radioactive dating shows that many fossils are millions of years old. Also, did you know that most stars we see are millions of light years away? How did the light from these stars get to the earth if the universe is only six thousand years old?

BINGO: Uhm, anyway, I think it's ridiculous to say man evolved from apes, because apes and humans are vastly different.

PROFESSOR: I don't think it's so ridiculous. If you compare the DNA of a man and a chimpanzee, you will find that they are 99 percent the same. Also, numerous fossils have been found of animals that were half ape and half man.

BINGO: Er, uhm, let me get back to you on that.

Bingo is starting to feel confused. He is starting to think that the arguments for evolution are stronger than the arguments for creation. This is

49

because Bingo doesn't know how to deal with the professor's arguments. It's not that Bingo's arguments for creation are bad, but that Bingo did not take the precaution of *anticipating opposing arguments*.

It is not good enough to have convincing reasons for the things you believe. If you want to have a strong position, then you need to anticipate opposing arguments and prepare counter arguments.

If all Bingo does is list the reasons why he believes in creation and finds lots of evidence why evolution is wrong, he is going to be shocked when he actually meets an evolutionist. Not only do evolutionists have good arguments for why they believe in evolution, but they also have some good arguments against creationism. If Bingo is going to win the argument with the professor, he needs to be aware of these arguments.

Tips

If Bingo had done a little research beforehand, he could have proven false, or at least countered, all of the professor's arguments against creationism. The Internet is a very useful tool for finding out what people believe and why. Bingo could find Web sites put up by evolutionists who disagree with creationism. Or he could visit his local library, which may have some books on the creation–evolution debate.

BINGO: Professor, I have been doing some research. There was no sun, but there was light on the third day. The ark was big enough. Cain married his sister. Radioactive dating has many assumptions. God created the stars so he can create light rays in transit. Ape-men fossils are bad science. The DNA of humans is 78 percent the same as a banana.

PROFESSOR: Er, uhm, let me get back to you on that.

Put Yourself in Their Shoes

If Bingo lives in the depths of the Peruvian rain forest, or is climbing one of the highest Himalayan mountains, where modern conveniences such as the Internet and local libraries do not reach, he could imagine himself in the place of someone who disagrees with creationism. What would that person say about his arguments? Bingo could have tried to argue with himself from the opposing side, trying to find flaws in his reasoning.

Your Argument Isn't That Great

"The first one to plead his cause seems right, Until his neighbor comes and examines him." (Proverbs 18:17)

Whatever Bingo's situation is, if he tries to anticipate some opposing arguments, his beliefs will actually grow stronger. He will gain a better perspective on his reasons for his beliefs.

We all have a tendency to imagine our own viewpoints to be much superior to those of everybody who disagrees. We think of ourselves as super geniuses who have an inside track on the truth. This isn't a good attitude.

Bingo found out that there are people who are more intelligent than he is, who have good arguments against his views about creation. This doesn't mean Bingo should change his views, but this experience has made Bingo a little more humble – and perhaps a little more careful.

In fact, the act of seriously trying to defeat our own arguments and anticipating arguments for the other side is very useful because it humbles us. We begin to realize that the reasons why we believe things might not be entirely based on good reasons.

Anticipate opposing arguments

1. **Research the subject.**

2. **Imagine yourself in the place of somebody who disagrees.**

Exercises

A. Below are stated viewpoints with some reasons in support of them. For each reason, anticipate some opposing arguments.

VIEWPOINT: Hiking in the Rocky Mountains is much more enjoyable than hiking in the Appalachian Mountains.

1. The Rocky Mountains are much taller than the Appalachians, which means the scenery is more beautiful.

2. The trees in the Rocky Mountains are pine trees. This means there is less poison ivy, and less underbrush when you are walking through the forest.

3. There are more rocks in the Rocky Mountains, and rocks are fun to climb on.

4. There are all kinds of abandoned mine shafts to explore which you can't find out east.

5. There is a greater variety of wildlife in the Rocky Mountains.

VIEWPOINT: Abortion is wrong.

6. The Bible, which is the Word of God, says that killing an unborn infant is murder. Also, the Bible says that murder is wrong.

7. It is clear from looking at ultrasounds of unborn infants that they can feel pain and react to stimuli, which indicates that they are alive, and not

just tissue – therefore abortion is also cruel.

8. For thousands of years, killing an unborn infant was considered murder.

9. I feel like it's wrong.

10. An unborn infant is alive; you can see it's alive!

VIEWPOINT: I think German Shepherds are the best kind of dogs to have.

11. They are big dogs, which is much better than having a scruffy little dog to trip over.

12. They can protect you from intruders.

13. They have pointy ears.

14. They are very intelligent.

VIEWPOINT: I believe that people who live south of the equator have opposite seasons from those who live north of the equator. I think when it's winter in Stockholm, Sweden, it's summer in Perth, Australia.

15. This is because the tilting of the earth causes the southern hemisphere to be away from the sun when the northern hemisphere is close to the sun. I read that in a book.

16. I know this is true because I read it in the encyclopedia.

17. It makes logical sense.

18. It's cold here right now, so it has to be warm somewhere else to even things out a bit and make it so only half the people on the earth are in misery.

Lesson 8

When Not to Use Logic

In a previous lesson we talked about how sometimes it is dumb to argue. We shouldn't argue when it would be socially inappropriate, when nobody knows much about the topic, or when one of the people involved is angry.

There are other times when we should not speak the logic in our heads – such as at a funeral.

Aunt Cynthia Pringle has died. The Littles are the Pringles' neighbors, and they are going to the funeral. Annette Pringle wants to take their dog Robey to the funeral. She wipes her eyes. "I know Robey wants to say goodbye to dear Aunt Cynthia."

Bingo Little feels he should say something: "Annette, Robey will probably be a nuisance at the funeral, and dogs can't understand what a funeral is, and Aunt

Cynthia never liked Robey anyway." This doesn't help. Annette gives Bingo a despairing look and runs back to her house.

Bingo feels bad. His older sister Bonnie suggests, "Sometimes we can help our friends by being quiet. If you offered to take Robey and watch him at the funeral, Annette might appreciate that."

We are glad Bingo sees the logic of the situation – that Robey should not attend the funeral. But sometimes a different logic takes precedence – the logic of human relationships and emotions. When we realize we should not speak our thoughts, we are not being illogical. We are being logical in silence.

To Speak or Not to Speak

Is it ever wrong to use logic?

At the funeral, Bingo overhears a conversation between his father and Uncle Pringle.

Uncle Pringle seems very upset, "I can't believe what's happened. What will I do without her? This isn't right. God could have taken anyone else. He didn't need to take my wife. It just isn't logical."

Mr. Little replies, "My mother died recently and I felt the same way. But you know, I've found some encouragement reading a book called . . ."

Mr. Little wants to help Uncle Pringle with some words of comfort. Sometimes this is more appropriate than to confront someone with his lack of logic. This is not what he needs.

The logic of the situation can overwhelm some of us. We feel we must speak out! Often this is not the way to help people. There is a time to speak logic, and there is a time to keep silent about logic.

If we feel logic pounding in our heads and demanding to be let out and say something that would hurt others, this is a lack of perspective, not logic. Knowing when to speak and when to be silent can be difficult.

It is never good to be illogical. But sometimes it is best not to speak aloud the logic in our minds.

However, there are times when we should speak out about logic.

Annette and Bingo are discussing logic. Annette says brusquely, "I just feel logic isn't for Christians. Did you know logic was invented by a pagan philosopher named Aristotle? Our pastor says modern Christians use logic to put God in a box instead of passionately embracing Him. I don't know what logic is, and I'm glad because not knowing helps me understand why it's so bad."

Bingo defends, "I think everybody uses logic – we can't communicate without it. And I read in a book that logic wasn't invented by Aristotle. It is written in our minds by God."

Exercises

A. In the following examples, choose the most appropriate response.

1. JUDDREY: Don't tell me to stop smoking. Look at you! You smoke seven packs a day, and the doctor says you have emphysema and should quit.

   a. BUBBA's: That's a logical fallacy . . . wheeze. . . . It's called Tu Quoque and it's when you accuse someone of doing what you're doing . . . wheeze.

   b. BUBBA's: You're right. I should stop smoking . . . wheeze. . . . Maybe you can help me.

2. SISTER: All boys are cavemen. If I hear another burp at the dinner table, I'm going on strike and I won't do any more of your cooking.

   a. BROTHER: Wait a second; I said 'excuse me' didn't I?

   b. BROTHER: I'll try not to burp. Sorry.

c. BROTHER: If you stop cooking, I'll stop carrying out the trash.

3. JOE: You must be colour-blind; your socks don't match.

   a. BOB: You misspelled the word "colour."

   b. BOB: Now that I look at them, I see they don't match.

   c. BOB: Just because my socks don't match doesn't mean I'm color-blind – or colour-blind.

4. NATHANIEL: We need to talk. This book isn't getting done. All the lessons don't fit together and nobody's listening to me and I've gotten nothing done today and I have a headache and I wish somebody would clean up the mess in the kitchen.

   a. HANS: You're just being illogical. I've gotten a lot done. You'd better make progress, or we won't meet our deadline.

   b. HANS: Looks like somebody's in a baaaaaad mooooood.

   c. HANS: Maybe you could take a walk outside. I'll clean up this mess.

5. DIETRICH: The Nazis are at the front door! What should we do with these Jews?

   a. CLAUS: We must logically consider the implications of hiding these Jews. If we tell the Nazis we have no Jews, we will be lying. But if we turn the Jews over to the Nazis . . .

   b. CLAUS: As it says in the book of Ecclesiastes, there is a time for words, and there is a time for action. We need to talk about whether this is a time for action or not. What do you say, Dietrich?

   c. Claus says nothing, but motions the guests to follow him into the secret room behind the fireplace.

6. JILL: I was at the farmer's market today – you knew it was today, didn't you – and I saw the strangest thing. This guy was selling sheep cheese! I didn't even know sheep made milk. I didn't try any; it smelled . . .

   a. JACK: The *Ovis aries* is a ruminant quadruped, and as such it would naturally feed its young with mammary secretions.

   b. JACK: What do you mean the cheese smelled? Did it crawl over to you and start sniffing?

c. JACK: I'm glad you didn't get that sheep cheese. It tastes worse than it smells.

7. LEHRER: Class, we've just listened to the Berlin Symphony Orchestra perform Mozart's "Eine Kleine Nachtmusik." Did you like it?

a. CLAUS: Mozart is all about logic. I've read that Mozart used mathematical equations when composing his music. That's why listening improves my IQ. I think Mozart marked the intellectual high point in musical development – things have gone downhill since.

b. HANS: That's not logical. There is no "high point" in music. Composers write music, and people like it or they don't. That's it. I can't stand it when people make dogmatic statements about some music being morally better and stuff.

c. GERTRUDE: It was okay. Can we listen to some bluegrass music now?

8. FRENCH MINISTER OF DEFENSE: We must go to war! The very idea of the Italian prime minister sending us a postcard with such an insulting joke! Our national pride is at stake!

a. FRENCH PRESIDENT: I agree! Why else was I elected but to protect our national sense of dignity!

b. FRENCH MINISTER OF FOREIGN AFFAIRS: Every civilized nation will stand behind us when we bomb Rome!

c. JANITOR: Sir, this card was postmarked in Baghdad. The Italian prime minister may not have sent it.

9. MARIE: Dear, we have a publishing deadline, and you're spending your time researching whether that guy on the talk show was right. Is this the best use of our time?

a. LESTER: You're probably right.

b. LESTER: But we can't allow bad logic to go undetected!

c. LESTER: I'm not wasting time . . . see, I've finished the first page in our book.

10. HANS: I'm worried about these two lessons. "When It's Dumb to Argue"

and "When Not to Use Logic" are very similar. They almost say the same thing.

a. NATHANIEL: That's not logical. There is a vast difference between the philosophical ramifications of arguing and the appropriate use of logic. I defy the proposition that argument is equal to logical strains of thought.

b. NATHANIEL: Ah, don't worry . . . no one will notice.

c. NATHANIEL: Maybe we could end the second lesson with a witty exercise admitting the lessons are similar. People won't mind.

11. Which of the following persons is being more logical?

a. LAMONT, DIRECTOR OF LIBRARY: A book has been stolen from The Large Letter Library; we have to find it. I don't think the stolen book is anywhere near the library. If the book were not in or near the library, then it would not have been found by now. It has not been found. This means it is not in or near the library. That's logic.

b. HEWEY: I disagree. If the stolen book were not in or near the library, then Marvin, the library cat, would have been mewing all day. He always does that when a book is gone that shouldn't be gone. Marvin has not been mewing. That means the book is in or near the library. That's better logic.

Tools for Opposing Viewpoints

Lesson 9

Using the Opposing Viewpoints Chart

One simple thinking tool which has many uses is a two-column chart. It looks like this:

Reasons to see Return of the Spatulas *tonight*

1. Reason 1

Reasons not to see Return of the Spatulas *tonight*

1. Reason 1

One of this chart's uses is to help you make a decision when you can't make up your mind. First you fill in the left column, then the right column.

1. It would be fun.
2. Tonight is the last night it will be playing.
3. All my friends are going to see it.
4. It's starring Christopher Crumb – my favorite actor.

1. I went out to a movie last night also; watching movies every night isn't good.
2. It's about spatulas, and spatula movies are always scary.
3. I have to finish writing this lesson in *The Thinking Toolbox* tonight.

While you still may not be able to make up your mind, at least now your thinking is clearer about the subject.

After you write the list, go through and cross off the reasons that are small or don't matter.

Reasons to see Return of the Spatulas *tonight.*

1. It would be fun.
2. Tonight is the last night it will be playing.
3. All my friends are going to see it.
4. It's starring Christopher Crumb – my favorite actor. [Cross off; maybe this isn't a good reason to go see a movie.]

Reasons not to see Return of the Spatulas *tonight*

1. I went out to a movie last night also, watching movies every night isn't good. [Cross off; I wouldn't be watching one every night, just last night and tonight. And besides, I could just say I won't watch a movie for a week after this.]
2. It's about spatulas, and spatula movies are always scary. [Cross off; I like having my socks scared off anyway.]
3. I have to finish writing this lesson in *The Thinking Toolbox* tonight.

Now the only reason against your going to the movie is the lesson you have to write. If you can arrange to write the lesson tomorrow, or write it before the movie, or if you are willing to stay up late, then it looks like you can go see the movie.

While using a chart isn't always the best way, sometimes this way of making decisions can be helpful.

This chart can be used for more things than just deciding whether to go to a movie. It can be useful when analyzing opposing viewpoints.

Opposing viewpoints *are two or more conflicting ideas, opinions, or points of view on one subject.*

For example, "Novels by Charles Dickens are always boring" and "Novels by Charles Dickens are exciting" are two points of view regarding Charles Dickens novels which contradict each other.

You can list reasons for each side on an *opposing viewpoints chart*. On one side of the opposing viewpoints chart you would put all the things that make Charles Dickens's novels boring, then on the other side, you (or somebody else) would put all the things which make Charles Dickens's novels exciting.

Novels by Charles Dickens are boring	*Novels by Charles Dickens are exciting*
1. They are long.	1. *A Christmas Carol* is fairly short.
2. They each have about a thousand characters whom you can never remember.	
3. They all contain lengthy sections of tedious dialogue.	
4. They always have some morbid lady who refuses to eat her wedding cake.	
5. I'd rather watch corn grow.	

As you can see, sometimes it is difficult to put things down on one side. This is because we are often emotionally biased toward one side or the other. We need to learn to look objectively at things – we need to be able to list things for an opposing side. No matter what our feelings are about the subject, we can always put *something* in both columns.

An Opposing Viewpoints Chart is useful for:

1. **Making difficult decisions.**

2. **Analyzing opposing viewpoints.**

3. **Objectively looking at issues with which we disagree.**

Exercises

A. Below are several pairs of opposing viewpoints. Create an opposing viewpoints chart for each pair and list several reasons in support of each view. Remember, you aren't deciding whether the reasons you put on each side are good or bad; you are just listing the reasons.

1. Homeschooling is good for children. Homeschooling is bad for children.

2. *Flight of the Phoenix* was a good movie. *Flight of the Phoenix* was not a good movie. (Substitute a movie you liked.)

3. The United States has a good form of government. The United States has a bad form of government. (If you are in a different country, substitute that country, if you aren't in any country at all, keep swimming.)

4. It would be good to live in Antarctica. It would not be good to live in Antarctica.

5. *Citizen Kane* was a boring movie. *Citizen Kane* was a good movie. (Substitute a movie you did not like.)

B. Are the following pairs of viewpoints opposing viewpoints?

6. Franklin Roosevelt was a good president. Franklin Roosevelt was not a

good president.

7. Michael Jordan can play basketball very well. Michael Jordan cannot play foosball very well.

C. Below is an opposing viewpoints chart. Which reasons here are bad, unimportant, or irrelevant reasons?

Robert E. Lee was a good general and a good man.

a. He was always a gentleman.
b. He fought for what he thought was right.
c. He looked better in gray than blue.
d. He didn't smoke.

Robert E. Lee was not a good general or a good man.

e. He fought for the South, and the South was for slavery.
f. Some of the men in his command owned slaves.
g. He fought in a war and killed people.
h. I still don't like the movie *Citizen Kane.*

Lesson 10

Opposing Viewpoints Are Everywhere

If we study any subject for very long, we will find that there are opposing viewpoints everywhere.

> KATHRYN: I've read two books on Clara Barton, and one said she was very shy and didn't talk much, and the other said she *wasn't* shy and talked a lot.

There are many periods of history where nobody really knows for sure what happened or what things were like. One history book will say Clara Barton was shy, and another will tell you that Clara Barton was definitely an extrovert – a fancy term for somebody who talks a lot. The trouble is, the authors of both books will sound authoritative – another fancy term for people who think there is nobody who disagrees with them – when nobody today really knows what Clara Barton was like.

So, if Kathryn had read only one book on Clara Barton, she would spend the rest of her life imagining Clara Barton as a shy person and not knowing that there are many historians who disagree.

While it may not be terribly important to know how much Clara Barton talked, there are many larger events in history where there are opposing viewpoints.

> FRANK: We've been studying in school about the Civil War. Yesterday we learned that the South was full of evil slave owners and that Abraham Lincoln invaded the South to free them from oppression. That is what the Civil War was about.
>
> BILLY: What? You're all wrong. It wasn't the "Civil War." It was "The War of Northern Aggression." We Southerners fought for states' rights and for freedom from the tyrants up north. But never fear, we'll beat you Yankees yet.
>
> FRANK: But the war ended in 1865.

BILLY: It isn't over. We're just reloadin'!

As you can see, there are some parts of history where viewpoints are very strong. Events such as the American Revolution, World War II, the assassination of John F. Kennedy, the death of Princess Anastasia, the gunfight at the O.K. Corral, and the Crusades all have many opposing viewpoints.

History isn't the only place where there are opposing viewpoints. There are also many in science.

MUSEUM TOUR GUIDE: Here we are standing next to the giant bones of the dinosaur Delopoticiciconianifesant Rex. This dinosaur lived in the early Emphasic period around two hundred forty-seven million seven hundred eighty thousand three hundred four years and seventy-six days ago. This dinosaur was known as a meat eater. Scientists can tell this because of the hungry look in his eye, known as the glutenounous look. This dinosaur probably died from suffocation as a result of being buried alive in rock. We know this because that is where we found him. We also know he is a male because he can't cook worth anything.

While not all scientists are this way, some scientists will make bold claims about things even though there are many people who disagree.

On any given topic there may be more than just two viewpoints.

SCIENTIST SAM: Gasses emitted out of the tailpipes of cars are causing global warming. Soon the polar ice caps will melt, and Los Angeles will go underwater.

SCIENTIST SUE: I disagree. Gasses emitted by cars aren't causing anything of the kind – they have virtually no effect on the temperature.

SCIENTIST SEDGWICK: I don't think we know for sure whether gasses emitted by cars are causing the earth to heat up. We should do more studies to find out.

What we need to remember when studying history, science, law, medicine, and virtually every other subject is that just because we read something in a book, that doesn't mean it's true. There may be other respected people who disagree with that book. We need to read other books and look at other viewpoints before we come to a conclusion.

In the next few lessons, we will be giving you some tools which will help you to look at opposing viewpoints.

There are at least two viewpoints on every issue.

Don't assume that the viewpoint you are reading about is the only one.

Exercises

A.1. Name three events in history or subjects in science where there are opposing viewpoints. Describe two of the different views.

B. In each of the following examples, name an opposing viewpoint.

2. German shepherds are a loyal breed of dog.

3. Democracy is a good, just, and efficient form of government – it is the best form of government.

4. Oliver Cromwell was the best ruler England ever had.

C. In each of the following examples, is there one character who *doesn't* disagree with the other two? Which one?

5. SCIENTIST SAM: I think humans evolved from animals into what they are now over millions of years. Our closest relative is the chimpanzee. There is a lot of archaeological evidence which agrees with this theory.
    SCIENTIST SUE: I think humans were created by God on one day a long time ago. And I don't think the archaeological evidence for your theory is very sound.
    SCIENTIST SEDGWICK: When are the doughnuts arriving?

6. JENNY: In 1492 Columbus landed in America. Before then, it was not widely known that the Americas existed.
    CLYDE: Actually, it was in early 1493.
    BERT: But the Vikings discovered America first, just not very many people knew about it.

7. FRED: Everybody living in southern Illinois is a hick.
    DERF: Most of the people in sorthern Illinois are hicks.
    ENROD: No, there are a lot of sophisticated people in East St. Louis, and that's southern Illinois.

8. FRED: Did you know William Shakespeare didn't write all those plays? It was really a guy named Sir Francis Bacon – he wrote all the plays and just put Shakespeare's name on them.
    DERF: That's ridiculous. Everybody knows Sir Francis Bacon was busy writing *The Lord of the Rings* at the time – he didn't have the time to mess around with a play.
    ENROD: I don't think Sir Francis Bacon was related to a pig.

9. FRANK: In the American Civil War, the North had a just cause. The South was only fighting to keep their slaves. God punished the South for their sins.
    BILLY: In the American Civil War, the South had a just cause. They were fighting for states' rights. The Union invaded the Confederate States of America (a separate country) because it was power-hungry.
    HANS: I think the war ended in 1865 and the North won, so I don't think it serves any purpose to keep arguing about it.

10. Which reasons given for the following viewpoints are bad, unimportant, or irrelevant?

There is a monster living in Lake Loch Ness, probably a plesiosaur.

    a. There have been a lot of people who say they have seen it.

    b. There are pictures of it.

    c. It would be really neat if there were one down there.

    d. It's possible.

There is no monster in Lake Loch Ness.

    e. The plesiosaurs died out a million years ago.

    f. All the sightings and photographs can be explained away.

    g. I've never seen it.

    h. Nobody has a real good picture of it.

    i. They haven't caught it yet and have no real proof.

    j. Rush Limbaugh doesn't think there is one down there.

Lesson 11

The Good, the Bad, and the Ugly Evidence

The opposing viewpoints chart is a useful tool, but how do we decide which side of the chart is stronger? How do we analyze the evidence?

Pringles on Vacation

The Pringle family has left on vacation. The Little family has agreed to care for the Pringles' dog, Robey, while they are gone.

While walking Robey, Bonnie Little notices that the Pringles left a light on in their house. Later that evening, she notices the light is turned off. This happens each day. The Little family is shocked one morning to see that the Pringles' yard has been mowed. Very odd. And the pile of newspapers on the Pringles' front porch is removed every couple of days. Also, someone put the trash out on Friday after the Pringles left. Very, very odd.

The Little family holds a family conference. Bonnie suggests that the Pringles never left on vacation. They are hiding in their house. This is an elaborate scheme to have someone else walk Robey. She points out that the word "vacation" can have a double meaning; the Pringle family may be taking a "vacation" from watching their complex little dog.

Do you think the Pringles have conspired to have the Littles take care of their dog? Bonnie made a list of the evidence.

Evidence for conspiracy

1. Light turned off
2. Yard mowed
3. Newspapers disappear
4. Trash taken out
5. Double meaning of "vacation"

Evidence against conspiracy

1. Pringles said they were on vacation

Compare the Evidence

When looking at an opposing viewpoints chart, often you will see more items in one column than in the other column. Does this mean that the column with more pieces of evidence is the better one? No. Some evidence is stronger than other evidence.

In our example, the Pringle family said they were going on vacation. This is a very a strong piece of evidence. Generally, we trust what people say.

If we look at the five pieces of evidence that Bonnie found for a conspiracy, we should notice that each one is weak. There may be an alternative explanation for why all of the mysterious things are happening. The evidence that the word "vacation" has a double meaning is very *speculative*.

The viewpoint which has the largest quantity of evidence isn't necessarily the correct viewpoint.

The End

Grandpa Pringle walks over to Bonnie and asks if he can borrow a rake. He complains about trimming the Pringles' grass, but says how glad he was he didn't have to babysit Robey. Grandpa Pringle said he picked up the newspapers and took out the trash. And the light was on an automated timer to keep burglars away.

In the following lessons, we will give you some tools for deciding whether evidence is strong or weak.

Exercises

A. In the examples below, choose which piece of evidence seems especially strong or especially weak when compared to the other evidence.

1. Bonnie thinks that Robey's excitableness stems from something in his diet.

   a. Robey loves to eat.

   b. Robey eats a special dog food made with organic meatballs.

   c. Every morning, before Bonnie takes him for a walk, the Pringles instructed her to give Robey his special treat called a "Zip and Zaz Cookie" made for older dogs that need more energy.

2. It is the Littles' turn to go on vacation, and Bingo Little is tired of sitting in the car as his family searches Prince Edward Island for the original

home of Anne of Green Gables. Bingo suggests no such house exists.

a. Bonnie is certain Green Gables is close. Everything looks very romantic – just like in the book.

b. The grass is very green and many of the houses have gables.

c. The book *Anne of Green Gables* can be found in the fiction section of the library.

3. Raymond the burglar has been watching the Pringles' house. He thinks it is safe to break in because he thinks the Pringles are on vacation. But his buddy Rufus disagrees.

a. The trash was taken out.

b. The light goes on and off like someone is in the house.

c. Raymond overheard Mrs. Pringle at the post office mention the word "vacation."

Lesson 12

You Can't Believe Everything You Hear

A source *is any place we get information about something. Books, newspapers, movies, the person next to you on the bus, and the label on your mattress can all be sources of information.*

When looking at sources, you will quickly realize that while some sources can be trusted, others cannot.

MAN ON INTERNET DISCUSSION BOARD: Did you know that the Queen of England doesn't need a driver's license to drive? She drives around all the time in her Range Rover without one.

This is quite an interesting thought. Why would the Queen of England not need a driver's license when everybody else does? But before we get carried away and start believing this, we need to ask a question.

US: How do you know that?

We shouldn't accept the claim of somebody on a discussion board just because he is saying something interesting or because we could imagine how it might be true – *anything* can be on a discussion board. We need to find out *how* he knows what he is saying is true. How do we know this man on the discussion board actually knows anything about the Queen of England?

MAN ON DISCUSSION BOARD: Uh, somebody told me about it. I think he read it on a Web site.

So, this man heard it from somebody else, who read it on an unknown

Web site. Should we trust him? Should we tell our friends that the Queen of England drives around without a license? Probably not. When sources tell us things, we need to be able to analyze them so that we can judge whether they are reliable.

There are rules for analyzing sources.

A Rule for Analyzing Sources:

If you don't know how a source obtained his information – how he knows what he knows – then the source should be considered unreliable.

When someone tells us something (like claiming that the queen doesn't need a driver's license), we should keep asking "Where did you hear that?" until we find out where that person obtained his information. If he cannot or will not tell us where he obtained his information, then all we have is that person's claim, and we should consider the information unreliable.

So, does the Queen of England need a driver's license to drive? We need to do a little research.

WWW.STRANGETHINGSABOUTFAMOUSPEOPLETHATYOUPROBABLYDONTKNOW-ABOUT.COM: One strange fact about Queen Elizabeth is that she doesn't need a driver's license to drive. In fact, she drives around all the time in her Range Rover. It even says so on the Royal Web site: "The queen doesn't need a driver's license to drive." Also, our reporter in England, Reginald Williams, said: "I've seen her drive in her Range Rover on several occasions."

This Web site seems as if it may be a slightly more credible source. However, we have not verified *this* Web site's source of information. We need to make sure the Web site's source says what it claims. It says the information came from the Royal Web site. We should check up on this as well.

WWW.ROYALBUCKINGHAMPALACEWEBSITE.UK: The Queen of England does not need a driver's license to drive.

www.royalbuckinghampalacewebsite.uk is probably a reliable source saying that the queen could drive a vehicle without a license *if she wants to*. It would know, and would probably have no reason to invent the idea. But the Royal Web site does not say that she actually *does* drive. When we check on sources we shouldn't assume things.

We could contact Reginald Williams from www.strangethingsaboutfamouspeoplethatyouprobablydontknowabout.com to find out if he actually did see the Queen driving around in a Range Rover.

But if we *really* wanted to know for sure, we could always go ourselves.

Late one night, you sneak into the Buckingham palace garage. You find a Range Rover parked there. It has a license plate that says "Warning: Queen in driver's seat." You hide in a garbage can. Early the next morning a lady walks in holding a handbag and wearing a crown. She gets in the driver's seat and drives away.

Exercises

A. 1. What is the first rule for analyzing sources?

B. In the following quotes, would you believe what the speaker is saying?

2. SALESMAN: For $87.98 this "Comfor-Zone" pillow will help you get a good night's sleep. You can take it from me, it works!

3. BUCKINGHAM PALACE GUARD: Ma'am, I would suggest that you do not enter this area, as it is a restricted zone and I will have to shoot you if you do.

4. MAN IN CROWDED PARKING LOT: Ma'am, are you having trouble finding a parking spot? You can leave the car with me and I'll park it for you. I'll bring it back to you when you need it, I promise.

5. GESTAPO AGENT: Your friend André has told us everysing, so you see it is pointless for you not to cooperate. All vee need from you is to confirm some minor facts zat vee know already. Tell us ze names of ze people in your resistance group.

6. *Encyclopedia Britannica*: The Tasmanian devil is a mammal of the marsupial family Dasyuridae, with a stocky body and large squarish head. The Tasmanian devil is 20 to 31 inches long. It has large jaws and strong teeth, and is named for its devilish expression, husky snarl, and often-bad temper.

7. If you wanted to know what the American Declaration of Independence said, which source would be more reliable?

   a. An American history book.

   b. The Declaration of Independence.

C. Decide whether the following e-mails should be forwarded. If you wanted to check up on these sources to find out if they were true, where would you go?

8. BILL GATES GIVES AWAY FORTUNE: Did you know that Bill Gates is giving away his massive fortune to anybody who wants to forward this

e-mail to their subscriber list? Yes, that's right, Bill Gates pledges to give you one hundred dollars for each person you forward this e-mail to. Why is he doing this? He says he is deeply grateful to all the people who have made him successful, and wants to give a little of his success back to his customers. All you have to do is send him the address you forwarded this to (so he can check if they are legitimate) and he will send you a check in the mail. Imagine, if you have only twenty people on your e-mail list you can make $2,000! But you don't have to take our word for it. The Microsoft Web site has confirmed this e-mail, saying it is legitimate, go there to check it out. So, forward this e-mail. . .hey, it couldn't hurt!

9. BOYCOTT KFC: During a recent study of KFC done at the University of New Hampshire, they found some very upsetting facts. First of all, has anybody noticed that just recently the company has changed its name? Kentucky Fried Chicken has become KFC. Does anybody know why? The reason is because they cannot use the word chicken anymore. Why? KFC does not use real chickens. They actually use genetically manipulated organisms. These so-called "chickens" are kept alive by tubes inserted into their bodies to pump blood and nutrients throughout their structure. They have no beaks, no feathers, and no feet. Their bone structure is dramatically shrunk to get more meat out of them. This is great for KFC because there is no more plucking of the feathers or the removal of the beaks and feet. The government has told them to change all of their menus so they do not say "chicken" anywhere. If you look closely you will notice this. Please forward this message to as many people as you can. Together we can make KFC start using real chicken again.

10. Find out on the Internet, or anywhere you choose, if the Queen of England drives without a driver's license. (By the way, the Web sites listed in this lesson do not exist.)

Lesson 13

Are You Primary or Secondary?

A primary source *is an eyewitness, somebody who saw an event with his own eyes or heard it with his own ears.*

A primary source is somebody who was there.

GREAT GREAT GRANDPA: Yep. I saw it with my own two eyes. I was young back in those days, 'bout fifteen. I was standin' back of the barn when I sees young Georgie – that's what we called him then – come round the corner with a hatchet. Then he commences hackin' away on that cherry tree. I don't know why he did it, didn't seem like his pa would care for him choppin' down the cherry tree. But he continues a hackin', smilin' all the while, till the little tree falls. Yep, I saw it happen all right.'

Great Great Grandpa is a primary source for what happened when the young George chopped down a cherry tree – he was there and actually *saw* the event himself.

If Great Great Grandpa didn't see the cherry tree chopped down himself, but heard about it from somebody else, he would be a *secondary source.*

A secondary source is not an eyewitness, but is someone who heard the story from somebody else.

PA: Yes, son, my great great grandpa told me all about what happened. Little George was there in front of his dad, when his dad says to him: "Son, do you know anything about my cherry tree out behind the barn? It seems somebody has chopped it down." Then George pipes up: "Father, I cannot tell a lie; I chopped down that cherry tree." "Okay, son," his father says, "go to the woodshed out back and cut for me a large switch. Your honesty surely won't save you from a thrashing."

Because he hadn't been born yet, Pa didn't actually see the scene he describes. However, he did hear about it from somebody else. Pa is a secondary source.

When we study history, there are many sources which tell us what happened at a particular event. Some of these sources are primary sources, and some of them are secondary sources.

When we read a history book, we often read an account written by somebody who was not there. The authors of history books will research an event, read about what happened, then write about it in their own words. It might come as a shock to you, but the things you read in a history book aren't necessarily true. They are often the author's interpretations of an event. This brings us to our second rule for analyzing sources.

Rule for Primary and Secondary Sources:

A primary source is generally more reliable than a secondary source because a story can change as it passes from one person to the next.

Historians believe that a primary source, who actually witnessed the event, is usually more accurate than a secondary source, who only heard it recounted. This is because each time somebody passes on a story to the next person, he might add a little bit to it.

> SON: George Washington was this really cool guy. My pa told me all about him. He said when George was seventeen years old, his dad gave him an axe that was seven feet long and weighed forty-two pounds. George chopped down twenty cherry trees with it, then told his dad. His dad got real mad at him and grounded him for a week.

This isn't exactly what his pa told him. This son is adding a few things to his father's story to make it more interesting.

This doesn't mean history books aren't useful to read. We should read a history book when we want to get an overview of what happened during an event. Sometimes watching a movie about an event may be a good idea. If the movie is good, it might get us excited about the event and the time period it is set in. We might go to the library and look up what really happened. However, when watching movies such as *Gone with the Wind* or *The Great Escape*, we have to be cautious. Movie makers want their movies to be dramatic and entertaining. They might make events in the past look more exciting than they really were.

Gossips – people who like to spread news about other people – are almost always secondary sources, because they usually repeat to others what they heard from cousin Nessie, who heard it from Ralph's sister, Margaret, who heard it from . . .

Exercises

A. 1.   What is the rule for primary and secondary sources?

B. Say whether each of the following examples is a primary or a secondary source.

2.   HISTORY BOOK: In the area west of the Mississippi from the period 1870-1892, often referred to as the "wild west," nearly everybody wore a gun – except Quakers and heroines. Saloons were often the scene of rough fist-fights. Men, often intoxicated, would throw other men through saloon windows or through swinging doors. Due to mislabeled shipments of balsa wood to the American west, chairs were also built to a much lower tolerance. During this period, black was the most popular color for hats, if you were a villain. Heroes most often wore white.

3.   "After we jumped into the water, it was every man for himself. I waded parallel to the beach with my squad because the heavy fire was directed towards the boats. As I was going straight towards the beach, I saw Lieutenant Hilscher go down on his knees as a shell exploded. He fell into the hole caused by the explosion. He died there on the beach. . . .When I finally reached the edge of the water, I started to run towards the seawall under a deafening roar of explosions and bullets. I saw a hole about seventy-five feet away, so I ran and jumped in, landing on top of O. T. Grimes." – Sergeant Warner Hamlett on D-Day, 1944.

4.   "Yes, sir. I was there. Leastways, my son was. Butch Cassidy came into the bank and said to the teller, "Hand over all the money, and nobody gets hurt." He had a bag in his hands and the teller commenced to fillin' it with bills. When he was done, Butch strolls out the door real cool-like. That man sure could rob a bank."

5.   "Here it comes, ladies and gentlemen, and what a sight it is, a thrilling one, a marvelous sight. The sun is striking the windows of the observation deck on the westward side and sparkling like glittering jewels on the background of black velvet. Passengers are looking out the windows

waving. The ship is standing still now. The vast motors are just holding it, just enough to keep from. . . . It's broken into flames! It's flashing . . . flashing! It's flashing terrible . . . oh, oh, oh! . . . It's burst into flames! . . . Oh my, this is terrible, oh my, get out of the way please! It is burning, bursting into flames and is falling. . . . Oh! This is one of the worst catastrophes in the world! Oh! It's a terrible sight. . . . Oh! and the humanity and all the passengers! I told you, it's a mass of smoking wreckage. Honest, I can hardly breathe. I'm going to step inside [the hangar] where I can't see it. . . It's terrible. I – I – folks, I'm going to have to stop for a moment because I've lost my voice. This is the worst thing I've ever witnessed." – Herbert Morrison, reporter for Chicago radio station WLS, describing the crash of the *Hindenburg* (May 6, 1937)

6. PROSECUTING ATTORNEY: Can you tell me what happened on the night in question, ma'am?
   MISS HOUSEMEN: Yes, I can. I was standing on the street corner when that man right there went into the bank. He had a gun in one hand and an empty bag in the other. A minute later I saw him coming out. He still had the gun, and the bag was full of money.

7. "About sixty-five million years ago a meteor about two miles wide struck the earth. The meteor's impact, followed by extended darkness from dust and debris thrown into the atmosphere, followed by more climate changes, weakened the last remaining dinosaurs to the point of extinction."

8. SAM: Did you know that the movie *The Great Escape* is a true story? I watched it last night. In it, Big X escapes from a German prisoner-of-war camp and then gets recaptured by the Gestapo.

9. *Encyclopedia Britannica*: The cheetah is a tawny-coated, black-spotted cat native to Africa and Southwest Asia, the fastest land animal, capable of running at speeds of up to seventy miles per hour.

Lesson 14

Who Has a Reason to Lie?

If you were a detective investigating a crime, it would be important to know if a witness was trustworthy. In our last lesson we learned that an eyewitness is generally more trustworthy than a newspaper article written by someone who was not there.

> DETECTIVE: Now, ma'am, can you tell us what happened?
> COOK: Yes, officer, I saw who stole the tarts.
> Most truly I tell you, it was the Knave of Hearts.
> He sneaked into the kitchen and stole those tarts.

News Flash: Knave of Hearts Swipes Some Tarts

> "A most terrible deed today was done.
> The Knave of Hearts made his way in and left not one.
> The Detective says he cannot find the plunderer:
> "I'm afraid the tarts are gone for good, he's probably eaten them by now."
> – *The Royal Enquirer*

The Detective regards the cook as a primary source. But why not question somebody the cook claims was there? The Knave of Hearts.

> THE KNAVE OF HEARTS: I did not steal those tarts on the plates.
> The one who says so prevaricates.

Wait a minute. The Knave of Hearts says he didn't steal the tarts. Should we believe him? Possibly not. The Knave of Hearts has a *reason to lie*.

Someone has a reason to lie *if he says things which make him look good or help his interests.*

Since the Knave of Hearts is suspected of a crime,
we should also suspect him of lying about it.

Crime suspects aren't the only ones who might have a reason to lie. Someone related to the person on trial, such as the mother of the Knave, might be motivated to lie to protect her son.

MOM: My son could never steal,
not even for a very good meal.

Anybody who is afraid he might be suspected of the crime may have a reason to lie.

GARDENER: I don't even like tarts.

People who have a reason to lie should be more suspect than people who don't. For example, politicians often have a reason to lie, so we should suspect what they tell us.

POLITICIAN: If you elect me to this title,
I promise you I will not be idle.
In this land I will reduce all such heinous crime,
For a just and honest man I'm.

Not only is this politician bad at creating rhymes but he also has a very good reason to lie about whether he is "a just and honest man" and whether he will be able to reduce crime – he wants to be elected.

It seems a bit unfair to the Knave to say he has a reason to lie, before we actually know whether he is guilty of the crime. However, when we say somebody has a reason to lie, we aren't actually saying he is lying; we are just putting a greater measure of suspicion on him. This brings us to another rule in analyzing evidence . . .

Rule for Reason to Lie:

We should prefer the testimony of somebody who does not have a reason to lie over somebody who does.

Who has a reason to lie?

1. **Does he say things that make him look good? Maybe they make him look brave, humble, or smart?**

2. **Does he say things which help his interests? Maybe they promote his business or keep him out of trouble.**

MAID: I was there with the cook.
I saw the Knave and what he took.

Since we know of no reason for the maid to lie, her testimony is strong.

However, when examining someone's testimony, it is important to be sure she really *doesn't* have a reason to lie. People who have something to hide often are very good at keeping it hidden. For example, the cook does not appear to have a reason to lie. However, if it were found out that the cook did not like the Knave of Hearts, we might want to suspect him of lying when he said he saw the Knave steal the tarts – we now know of a reason for him to lie.

Sometimes, we can be fairly certain there is no lying going on.

DETECTIVE: Do you know anything about this crime?
SEVEN OF CLUBS: Oh, yes, I must confess,
Of this situation, I have made a mess.
When I knew Knave of Hearts had stolen those tarts,
I went to him and asked him if I might have some parts.

Don't you wish everybody was this honest? The Seven of Clubs would have benefited if he had lied about what had happened. But it is unlikely that he is lying because he says things which hurt his own interests – he confesses that he is partially culpable in the crime. If what someone says actually hurts his interests, he has no reason to lie, so his testimony is very strong.

Exercises

A. 1. What is the rule for Reason to Lie?

B. In the examples below, decide if the witness has a known reason to lie. Why?

2. DETECTIVE: Sir, the cook says the Knave of Hearts did it. Can you tell me what you saw?
KNAVE OF DIAMONDS: I was in the garden when I saw the Knave.
He was covered with crumbs.
Yes, he had crumbs on both his thumbs.

3. BERT: Let's go to see The Flying Bumpkins tonight.
SCOTTY: I don't know. My mom doesn't like me seeing movies that have flying creatures in them.
BERT: Aw, it's not about flying creatures. "Flying" only means they run

very fast.

4. GENERAL TO HIS TROOPS: I am afraid, men. I am afraid of tomorrow's battle. It appears the enemy is too strong for us. I fear that we will be massacred.

5. "John Smith is a candidate who can energize people to get to the polls, a candidate who can raise the money to be heard, and a candidate who can draw clear distinctions between himself and the opposing candidate. That is why the Worker's Union is supporting John Smith." – Andrew Jones, President of Worker's Union

6. "The green mamba is the [most] dreaded snake species of Africa. Treat it with great respect. It is considered one of the most dangerous snakes known to man. Not only is it highly venomous, but it is aggressive and its victim has little chance to escape from a bite." – *The Illustrated Guide to Poisonous Snakes*

7. "The Gold Market, which is currently at $386 an ounce, is predicted by experts to have the explosive upside potential of reaching up to $1,500 an ounce." – United States Rare Coin & Bullion Reserve (which sells gold coins)

8. "As a whole, the [Russian] armed forces are only 75-80 percent equipped with fully functioning ammunition and technology, and of this, modern weapons make up less than 20 percent." – Russian Defense Minister Sergei Ivanov

9. ELY: Do I believe in aliens from other planets? I sure do. I've seen 'em. I was standing out on my back porch one day when I saw this big hovering saucer. It landed in my backyard. A door opened up, and these little green men came down a ladder. They walked up to me and asked me in squeaky voices if there were any good Chinese buffets in the area. I told them about the one around the corner and they said "thank you" – real polite-like – got back in their machine and flew off. Yes, sir. I've seen aliens. I sent my story to this UFO magazine, and they printed it.

10. "Photographic Memory Pills are much better than Superthinker Pills. They have helped enormously with my memory retention. My wife told me, 'You didn't forget our anniversary this year.'" – Carl Reno, president of Photographic Memory Pills, Inc.

C. In the following examples, identify any known reason for the source to be questioned for reliability.

11. "Did you know that you don't have to pay income tax? It's all a scam by the IRS. There really isn't a law that says you have to pay income tax. I know the IRS will try to tell you there is a law, but if you actually look for the law, you won't find it."

12. OFFICER CARSON: My radar is busted, but it looked like you were going pretty fast back there. How fast were you going?
MOTORIST: Sorry, officer, I was going 56 and the speed limit was 45. I was speeding.

13. PROSECUTING ATTORNEY: Mr. Fallon, you must know your wife very well and love her very much. She has been accused of murder. Is she capable of it?
MR. FALLON: I'm really sorry to say it, as much as I love her and all, but she's somebody you don't want as an enemy. I can easily see her bumping off anybody who got in her way.

14. HISTORY BOOK: People of early colonial America loved music, singing, and dancing. These diversions were prohibited in certain areas for religious reasons, but people found ways to enjoy these amusements despite the restrictions.

15. "Black men in service to the South were such common sights that, not only did Northern officers and enlisted men write about the service to the South by blacks, but also a British officer reported on the service rendered the South by its black soldiers." – from a book called *The South Was Right!*

16. "I've tried other memory supplements before, but the day I started using Superthinker Pills, I noticed a difference. Now I don't forget things. I can finally remember where I put my keys. Superthinker Pills are better than Photographic Memory Pills." – Sam Sparks, postal worker

Lesson 15

Corroborating Evidence

SHERIFF: The bank was robbed yesterday evening by a guy who fits your description. Did you do it?

RUSTY: I wasn't anywhere near the bank yesterday evening, sheriff.

If we know someone has a reason to lie, then we should closely examine his story and look for other evidence which agrees with what he says. We call this *corroborating evidence.*

Someone has corroborating evidence *when there are other witnesses, records, or evidence which supports the same idea.*

If Rusty were accused of a crime which he did not commit, then he would like somebody to come forward and say that he was somewhere else at the time the crime was committed.

That person would be corroborating Rusty's story.

BARBER: That's right. He was with me in the barber shop getting his hair cut!

The barber is corroborating Rusty's story. In the sheriff's eyes, the barber makes Rusty's story stronger and more believable. Rusty couldn't have been robbing a bank and getting his hair cut at the same time.

Corroborating evidence does not have to be in the form of another witness. It can be found in physical evidence as well.

DEPUTY: Look there! There's some of Rusty's hair lying on the floor of the barber shop. That seems to indicate that he was here last night.

Notice how that last piece of evidence doesn't necessarily mean that Rusty was in the barber shot last evening (the hair could have been planted there or fallen there earlier in the day), but it does support his story.

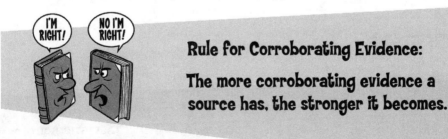

Rule for Corroborating Evidence:

The more corroborating evidence a source has, the stronger it becomes.

This means the more witnesses and bits of evidence Rusty can find which seem to indicate that he was in the barber shop at the time of the crime, the stronger Rusty's story becomes in the eyes of the sheriff. Other pieces of evidence which would corroborate Rusty's story could include a receipt from the barber dated at the time of the robbery, another person in the barber shop who saw him at that time, or the fact that Rusty's hair appears to have been recently cut.

Sometimes a corroborating witness cannot do very much for the person he corroborates. If someone is being accused of a crime, then he has a reason to lie. If his corroborating witness is also being accused of the crime, then he also has a reason to lie. Both suspects are still on shaky ground.

> SHERIFF: Where were both of you last night around seven o'clock?
> SCAR FACE: I was outside of town sleeping in the sagebrush.
> DEADEYE DAN: That's true. I can corroborate his story, I was there with him.
> SCAR FACE: Yeah, and I can corroborate that Deadeye Dan didn't rob the bank either; he was in the sagebrush with me.

Exercises

A. 1. What is the rule for Corroborating Evidence?

B. Below each quote or story are some pieces of evidence. Say whether the piece of evidence corroborates the quote.

> RUSTY: It wasn't me who robbed the bank yesterday evening. It was Scar Face.

I saw him do it. I was sitting in the barber's chair, getting my hair cut, when I sees Scar Face and his pal Deadeye Dan go into the bank with guns drawn. They came out a little while later with bags of money.

2. Scar Face's fingerprint was found on the bank's safe.

3. URANIUM URIAH: There weren't just one feller who robbed that bank. I saw two go in. I was in the general store getting supplies when I sees two people go into the bank. Then they comes out with bags of money.

4. Molly Brown up the street did not see Rusty go into the bank last evening.

5. Scar Face and Deadeye Dan were seen by witnesses this morning at the general store buying a set of expensive clothes, two pearl-handled six-shooters, and two cases of Dutch chocolates.

6. Deadeye Dan says he was over in the saloon when the robbery happened.

7. The saloon keeper says Deadeye Dan was in his saloon yesterday evening.

Before alligators were protected by law, you could buy baby ones in Florida and Georgia for a few dollars as a souvenir. Many were sold without any regard to how difficult a pet an alligator would make. In New York City alone, hundreds of these small 'gators were flushed down toilets or set free to eventually end up in the city's sewer system. The baby 'gators adapted to this environment quickly by feeding on rats and other sewer dwellers. Generations later, these alligators became albino and went blind from the lack of light. Also, they grew very large with no competition from other predators. Occasionally sewer workers and bums will disappear when the rat supply dwindles.

8. Joe the cab driver says he once saw an alligator in a sewer. "It was big and white. It had the largest teeth you could imagine."

9. Over the past year, the population of rats in New York has dwindled.

10. There have been reports of crocodiles living in the sewer systems of some Indonesian cities.

11. The New York City health department denies that there are any alligators living in the sewer system.

12. An expedition led by the famous explorer Cal Thortelmung ventured

into the sewer systems of New York but found no alligators. "It was pretty dark down there. They could be living in there, but we didn't see any. I wish I had brought a flashlight."

13. Barbara from Muskogee, Oklahoma, thinks that there probably are alligators living in New York.

14. A dead alligator was found lying beside the track along a subway line last April.

C. In the following examples, find any known reason for the source to be questioned for reliability.

15. "Homeschooled children and youth develop strong ties with their parents and siblings. Research shows that they are also socially, emotionally, and psychologically healthy and strong." – *Worldwide Guide to Homeschooling* by Brian D. Ray, Ph.D., head of National Home Education Research Institute

16. "Sir Knight, I know not who thou art, but I do pledge my knightly word that thou art the most potent knight that ever I have met in all my life." – King Arthur

17. HISTORY BOOK: During the early years of colonization in America, the first settlers worked hard and faced many difficulties. They hoped to create a better way of life for themselves in the colonies.

18. "I've been taking Focus Factor since we introduced it two years ago. I wouldn't work a day without it." – Rob Graham, president of Focus Factor

19. "Queen Elizabeth learned to drive during WWII as a young volunteer in the army, and she still drives her own stick-shift Land Rover when she's at Balmoral, her country estate in Scotland."

Lesson 16

Mystery of the Stolen Manoot

Mrs. McLeary lives in a large house in the country with a large staff of servants. Her prized possession is the painting *The Picnic* by Manoot. While everybody knows the picture is worth practically nothing, she considers it priceless. She keeps the painting hanging in the library. Every night she ensures all the doors of the house are locked.

On Monday night, Mrs. McLeary's painting was stolen from her library wall. While the painting is insured, Mrs. McLeary still wants it recovered.

Constable Dobson has been called in to investigate. Upon arriving, Constable Dobson gathered some clues.

1. He noticed that the library window has been forced.
2. The picture frame, without the picture in it, was found in the bushes near the house.
3. A vagrant named "Pinkie" was found loitering around the

McLeary mansion. He was arrested for stealing the painting.

Constable Dobson then asked some questions, and heard the following:

BRINCKLEY, THE BUTLER: I slept soundly, sir, and so have nothing useful to convey regarding the night's proceedings. However, sir, yesterday afternoon, when I was in the garden, I chanced to encounter the vagrant known as "Pinkie" upon the grounds. I caught him in the act of peering into one of the library windows. I thought the information might be useful in your investigation, sir.

MRS. MCLEARY: I can't believe it's gone! My precious painting! But I know who stole it. It was that vagrant. I know because I saw him at it. I got up in the middle of the night to get a drink of water. When I was going back to bed I looked out the window. I saw a man on the lawn – he looked like a vagrant. He was running away with a large square object under his arm. I didn't think anything about it until I came downstairs this morning and my painting was gone.

On the way to the police station, Constable Dobson met Mrs. Norton, Mrs. McLeary's neighbor.

MRS. NORTON: So, somebody finally pinched that monstrosity of a painting. If you ask me, I think the old buzzard stole it herself. She just wants to collect on the insurance. Everybody knows that she is hard up for money these days. If she doesn't collect the insurance money, she'll have to sell the house.

PINKIE THE VAGRANT: I haven't done nothin'. It weren't me who took it, it was that Mrs. McLeary. Last night, I was lying in the bushes, tryin' to get an honest man's sleep, when I saw 'er comin' through a window with a picture under 'er arm. Breakin' out of 'er own 'ouse didn't seem natural, so I kept lookin'. She came over to the bushes and took that frame off the picture, and threw it in the bushes. Then she walked off. I don't know what she did after that.

Exercises

A. Answer the following questions about each of the witnesses. Please stick only to what you know about the case, not things you imagine could be true.

The object right now isn't to solve the mystery, but to evaluate the stories.

1. Is Brinckley the Butler a primary source?

2. Who does Brinckley suspect of the theft?

3. Do you know of a reason for Brinckley to lie?

4. Is there any corroborating evidence for Brinckley's story?

5. Would you consider Brinckley a reliable source ?

6. Is Mrs. McLeary a primary source?

7. Do you know of a reason for Mrs. McLeary to lie?

8. Is there any corroborating evidence for Mrs. McLeary's story?

9. What are two things which make Mrs. McLeary's story unreliable?

10. Do you think Mrs. McLeary is a reliable source?

11. Is Mrs. Norton a primary source?

12. Do you know of a reason for Mrs. Norton to lie?

13. Is there any corroborating evidence for Mrs. Norton's story?

14. Is Pinkie the Vagrant a primary source?

15. Do you know of a reason for Pinkie the Vagrant to lie?

16. Is there any corroborating evidence for Pinkie the Vagrant's story?

17. Do you think Pinkie the Vagrant is a reliable source?

18. What do you think Constable Dobson should do now?

Lesson 17

Stir Plot until Thickened

Back at the mansion, Mrs. McLeary seems distraught over the loss of her painting.

MRS. MCLEARY: Constable, I insist that you do something to recover my painting. I am telephoning my son, Fonsworth, to come down from London by the first train. If something isn't done soon, I will tell him to bring a private detective.

Do you have any suggestions for Constable Dobson?

"I think the window area as well as the picture frame should be dusted for fingerprints." – Karen S.

Good idea. Constable Dobson went to the library with his brush and baby powder and started dusting. Unfortunately, the results only turned up a few fingerprints on the window sill and one or two on the recovered picture frame; all of them were from either Mrs. McLeary or Brinckley the Butler.

BRINCKLEY THE BUTLER: Mrs. McLeary and I are the only persons allowed to handle the paintings, sir. It is my duty to dust them every morning, and Mrs. McLeary makes occasional adjustments.

CONSTABLE DOBSON: Is the picture that was stolen very different from the rest of the paintings?

BRINCKLEY THE BUTLER: Yes sir. Mrs. McLeary's other paintings were inherited from the family collection, but the particular painting in question, *The Picnic* by Manoot, was purchased by Mrs. McLeary about a year ago, sir. As you can see, the original paintings are from a more classical period, while *The Picnic* was of a somewhat, shall we say, "modern" taste.

CONSTABLE DOBSON: You seem to know a lot about paintings.

BRINCKLEY THE BUTLER: Yes, sir. I fancy myself somewhat of a connoisseur. I have been responsible for the collection for many years, even preceding the current Mrs. McLeary's ownership.

Do you have any other suggestions?

"We were told the painting is worth practically nothing; what was its insured value?" – Julie L.

INSURANCE COMPANY: That particular painting was appraised at a very low value and, therefore, could not be insured. However, there is a large insurance policy on the picture frame that the painting was in. The frame is very old and of Italian design, and so it would command a high price on the art market.

So, the picture isn't insured; it's the *frame* that is insured!

MRS. MCLEARY: I want you to know, Constable, that no insurance company in the country could insure my Manoot for what it is truly worth.

BRINCKLEY THE BUTLER: Excuse me, Constable; Mr. Fonsworth has now arrived. Is it your desire to speak with him for the purpose of gaining necessary information?

CONSTABLE DOBSON: Huh, what? Oh yes! Show him in.

FONSWORTH MCLEARY: What's this all about? Some poor chap made off with mother's cherished painting, what? Poor burglar doesn't know what he's in for. I can imagine his face when he looks at the thing in broad daylight; it's enough to curdle blood.

Constable Dobson: So you would not say the painting is beautiful?

FONSWORTH: Beautiful? No! The thing looks as though it were created by a inebriated orangutan on the back of a camel.

CONSTABLE DOBSON: Indeed! Have you any idea who might have stolen it?

FONSWORTH: No idea who would want the thing. As I told you, one look at that ghastly thing will knock at least a week off your life.

Interesting. What do you think the constable should do next?

"Has the constable conducted a search of the entire house to look for the painting?" – Anni W.

BRINCKLEY: Constable, I believe a search would at this time be unnecessary as the painting, or rather what remains of the painting, has been recovered.

CONSTABLE DOBSON: What? Where?

BRINCKLEY: Yes, sir. The maid discovered a charred corner a few moments ago in the library fireplace. She recognized it by its peculiar color, sir.

Exercises

A. Now it is your turn to solve "The Mystery of the Stolen Manoot." Who stole the painting and burned it in the fireplace? Explain why.

HINT: You have all the information necessary. To solve the mystery, decide who has the strongest motive for the crime. Nobody in "Stir Plot Until Thickened" is lying.

Below is a list of the possible suspects.

1. Fonsworth W. McLeary (son of Mrs. McLeary) – Thirty-something. Friendly and happy-go-lucky. Had Danish and tea for breakfast.
2. Brinckley the Butler – Over fifty. Calm and cool. Disciplined. Apt to use elaborate language. Sensitive in matters of taste. Had "Bacon and eggs, sir" for breakfast.
3. Mrs. McLeary – Over sixty-five. Interested in art, but with odd taste. A little excitable and imaginative. Had nothing for breakfast; too upset.
4. Mrs. Norton – Around fifty. Appears to dislike Mrs. McLeary. Intelligent. Gardens as a hobby. Had a bagel with cream cheese for breakfast.
5. Pinkie the Vagrant – Age: Unknown. Uses bad grammar. Curious. Not overly intelligent, but able to put two and two together. The jailer gave him bacon and eggs for breakfast.

For the solution to "The Mystery of the Stolen Manoot," see the Answer Key.

Lesson 18

Gunfight at the O. K. Corral

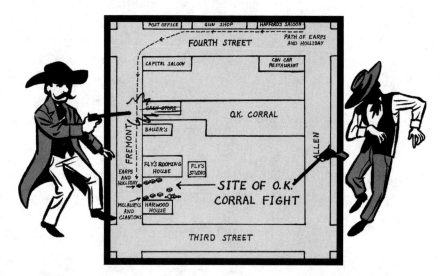

Tombstone, Arizona, October 26, 1881. City Marshall Virgil Earp suspected trouble was brewing with the Clanton bunch down by the O. K. Stable lot. Rumor had it they were armed and were preparing for a fight.

The Earp brothers – Virgil, Wyatt, and Morgan – and Doc Holliday walked up Fremont Street to an abandoned lot near O. K. Corral to disarm the Clantons. There they met Billy and Ike Clanton and Tom and Frank McLaury. City Marshal Virgil Earp demanded that the cowboys surrender. They didn't. In about forty seconds, thirty shots were fired, and the two McLaurys and Billy Clanton were dead, and Doc Holliday, and Virgil and Morgan Earp were wounded.

Days later, Wyatt Earp and Doc Holliday were charged with murder. Your job: Are they guilty?

The Gunfight at the O. K. Corral is probably the most famous gun battle of the Wild West. It has been recounted in numerous movies, TV programs, and novels, most of which portray the Earp boys as tough, handsome lawmen upholding the peace. Was this true? You will see evidence on both sides of the shootout. Your job is to use critical thinking tools to decide whether the killings of the McLaurys and Billy Clanton were justifiable acts of self-defense . . . or murder.

Wyatt Earp

Meanwhile, back at the O. K. Corral. . .
Wyatt Earp had this to say about the shootout:

"[Frank and Tom McLaury, Billy Clanton, and] Ike Clanton stationed themselves on a fifteen foot lot between two buildings across the street and sent us word that if we did not come down there and fight they would waylay and kill us. So we started down after them – Doc Holliday, Virgil, Morgan, and I. As we came to the lot, they moved back and backed against one of the buildings. "I'm going to arrest you boys," said Virgil. For answer, their six-shooters began to spit. Frank McLaury fired at me and Billy Clanton at Morgan. Both missed. I had a gun in my overcoat pocket, and I jerked it out at Frank McLaury, hitting him in the stomach." – Wyatt Earp in the *San Francisco Examiner,* August 2, 1896

Wyatt's statement said three things about the O. K. Corral gunfight:

1. The Clanton bunch threatened to kill one or more of the Earp brothers.
2. Before the fight started, Virgil Earp tried to arrest them peacefully.
3. The Clanton bunch fired first, and the Earps and Doc Holliday fired in self-defense.

There are three things people disagree about:
1. Whether the Clantons threatened the Earps beforehand.
2. Whether the Earps gave the Clantons enough warning.
3. Who fired first?

What are the strengths and weaknesses of Wyatt's testimony?

Strengths: Since Wyatt was there and saw the gunfight, he is a primary source. In fact, since he was involved with the gunfight, he had a very good view to see what happened. Since this fight took place very quickly, somebody who wasn't very close to the action might not have some important details. Wyatt was also a peace officer. This means he had some authority and was probably a trusted member of the community.

Weaknesses: Since Wyatt was on trial for murder, he had a very good reason to lie about what happened. He had a good reason to say he and his brothers shot in self-defense.

This second account is from John P. Gray, a bystander who saw the shoot-out.

John P. Gray

"The three Earps – Wyatt, Virgil, and Morgan – and Doc Holliday had stepped suddenly out on to Fremont Street from the rear entrance of the O. K. stable lot and immediately commenced firing on the cowboys who were preparing to leave town. . . . It was over almost as soon as begun. A play enacted by the Earps to wipe out those cowboys on the pretense of enforcing the law – and carried out under the manner of shooting first and reading the warrant to the dead men afterward. But in this case, I doubt if there was ever a warrant issued. The Earps called out, 'Hands up' and began firing almost simultaneously." – John P. Gray

Exercises

A. Answer the following questions about Mr. Gray's testimony.

1. Is Mr. Gray a primary source?

2. What did he say was his vantage point on the view of the shootout? Does he say he had a good view to see everything that happened?

3. Does Mr. Gray mention any threat by the Clantons to kill the Earps?

4. What does Mr. Gray say about the intentions of the Clanton bunch before the shootout started?

5. Does Mr. Gray mention anything about the Earps' attempt to disarm the cowboys?

6. Who does Mr. Gray say fired first?

7. Do we know of any reason for Mr. Gray to lie?

8. Which side does Mr. Gray's story corroborate: the Earps' side or the Clantons' side?

9. What makes Mr. Gray's story strong; what makes it weak?

B. Who fired first? Below are some eyewitness accounts of either the gunfight or events surrounding it. For each of the pieces of evidence below, what does the witness say about: (1) Who fired first? (2) Did he or she have a good view to see everything that happened? (3) Does the witness have a reason to lie?

10. "I think it was Holliday who fired first. Their backs were to me. I was behind them. The smoke came from him. I could not tell who fired the second shot." – William Allen, bystander

11. "The first two shots were fired by Holliday and Morgan Earp. . . . Morgan Earp shot [Billy] Clanton, and I don't know which one of the McLaury boys Holliday shot at. He shot at one of them." – Ike Clanton, participant

C. Did the Earps give enough warning? For each of the pieces of evidence below, what does the witness say about: (1) Did the Earps give enough warning? (2) Did he or she have a good view to see everything that happened? (3) Does the witness have a reason to lie?

12. "As soon as I saw them, I said, 'Boys, throw up your hands, I want your guns, or arms.' With that Frank McLaury and Billy Clanton drew their six-shooters and commenced to cock them, and I heard them go 'click-click.' Ike Clanton threw his hand in his breast, this way. At that, I said throwing both hands up, with the cane in my right hand, 'Hold on, I don't want that!' – Virgil Earp

13. "I saw a nickel-plated pistol in particular which was pointed at one of the party. I think at Billy Clanton. My impression at the time was that Holliday had the nickel-plated pistol. After the remark 'Throw up your hands!' was made, the nickel-plated pistol went off." – John Behan, sheriff

14. Mrs. King saw the Earp party as they approached the vacant lot before the shootout. This is what she said: "I saw four men coming down the sidewalk. I only knew one of the party, and that was Mr. Holliday. And there were three other gentlemen, who someone told me were the Earps. Mr. Holliday was next to the buildings, on the inside. He had a gun under his coat. . . . I stood in the door until these gentlemen passed and until they got to the second door. . . . I heard this man on the outside – he looked at Holliday and I heard him say, 'Let them have it!' And Doc Holliday said, 'All right.'" – Mrs. King

D. Did the Clantons threaten the Earps before the fight? For each of the pieces of evidence below, what does the witness say about: (1) Was there any threat to the Earps before the fight? (2) Does the witness have a reason to lie?

15. Town Marshal Virgil Earp, in his testimony during the trial, told of an incident which happened earlier in the day: "I found Ike Clanton on Fourth Street between Fremont and Allen with a Winchester rifle in his hand and a six-shooter stuck down his breeches. I walked up and grabbed the rifle in my left hand. He let loose and started to draw his six-shooter. I hit him over the head with mine and knocked him to his knees and took his six-shooter from him. I asked him if he was hunting for me. He said he was, and if he had seen me a second sooner he would

have killed me. I arrested Ike for carrying firearms . . . inside the city limits." [Public court documents recorded that day show that Ike Clanton was arrested and fined $25 for carrying a concealed firearm.]

16. "I walked from the corner of Fourth and Allen Streets, west, just across the street. J. L. Fonck met me there, and he said, 'The cowboys are making threats against you.' . . . I told him I would not bother them as long as they were in the corral – if they showed up on the street, I would disarm them. 'Why,' he said, 'they are all down on Fremont Street there now.' Then I called on Wyatt and Morgan Earp and Doc Holliday to go with me and help disarm them." – Virgil Earp

17. "[Earlier] when Holliday and the Earps appeared on the streets, he [Ike Clanton] repeatedly cried, "The ball will open." He had also paid an early morning visit to Fly's Rooming house hunting Doc Holliday with a rifle and a six-shooter." – Kate Elder, citizen and friend of Doc Holliday

18. Write a short paragraph describing what you think happened during the Gunfight at the O.K. Corral. Give evidence to support your opinion.

References

Die in the West: The Story of the O.K. Corral Gunfight by Paula Mitchell Marks (William Morrow and Co., Inc., 1989).

The Earps Talk edited by Turner E. Alford (Creative Pub. Co., 1982).

The Gunfighters by Paul Trachtman (Time-Life Books, 1974).

Inventing Wyatt Earp, His Life and Many Legends by Allen Barra (Carroll & Graf Publishers, Inc., 1998).

Tombstone: Myth and Reality by Odie B. Faulk (Oxford University Press, 1972).

Lesson 19

Does a "Possibly" Make a "Probably"?

In a previous lesson, we explained how to compare the evidence on both sides of an opposing viewpoints chart. Often, what matters is the quality of evidence, not the quantity. We would like to explain another mistake people make. We call it the *possibility fallacy*.

The possibility fallacy *is confusing something that is only possible with something that is probable.*

Special Report: Moon Landing Hoax

In 1969, NASA announced they had landed a man on the moon. However, there is growing evidence that this was a hoax.

It started when veteran photograph analyzer "Allan" began to question whether it was possible to land on the moon. "I found we couldn't have done it," he said. "The technology just wasn't there in 1969. Computers were merely glorified calculators.'

"But what about the pictures of astronauts on the moon?" you ask. Allan and his team studied the Apollo photographs and concluded, "There are literally tons of problems. Our discoveries suggest these pictures were actually taken in a Hollywood studio."

For example, look at Photo A.

Photo A

Where are the stars? ". . . on the moon there isn't any atmosphere, so you should see more stars than on Earth. But we can't see a single star!"

Now look at Photo B.

Photo B

Do you see the "C" someone drew on the rock? This probably meant the rock went in a certain place on the stage – they just forgot to turn it upside down.

Another question Allan asks is, "How is it possible that they took so many pictures? The average temperature on the moon during the day ranges from 260° F to 280° F. How did the film in the cameras survive? At that temperature, photographic film would melt."

Why did NASA fake the moon landings? Allan says the answer is simple. "We were in the Cold War with Russia, and we wanted to show the world that we were better."

Did This Report Convince You?

This report shows us it is *possible* the NASA moon landing was a hoax. (1) Maybe we can't see the stars because it was all faked. (2) Maybe there's a "C" on the rock because it was a studio prop. (3) Maybe the film would melt if it were taken to the moon. So, it is possible NASA didn't land on the moon.

But remember, a "possibility" doesn't make a "probability." There is a lot of evidence that NASA did land on the moon. Let's list the evidence in an opposing viewpoints chart.

Evidence NASA didn't land on the moon	*Evidence NASA did land on the moon*
1. We can't see the stars in the pictures.	1. All the photos and videos are evidence.
2. There is a "C" on the rock.	2. Astronauts alive today claim they walked on the moon.
3. The film (not to mention the astronauts.) would have melted in the extreme heat.	3. Hundreds of scientists worked on the Apollo program. None of them say it was a fake.
4. The United States government wanted to beat Russia to the moon, so they had a reason to lie about it.	4. Today scientists can study moon rocks which the astronauts brought back. These rocks are different from anything found on earth.
	5. NASA has explained all the anomalies found in the photos.

We commit the possibility fallacy when we look at the evidence in the first column and become curious. We see it is possible that the moon landings were faked. Then we become so excited that we imagine the evidence is probably true!

Difference between "Possible" and "Probable"

All of us can confuse these important ideas: (1) what is impossible, (2) what is possible, and (3) what is probable. Let's explain the difference.

1. Something is *impossible* if there is no way for it to be true.

Jack realized he'd made a revolutionary discovery. "When you add two plus three underwater, you always come up with seven. Every math textbook should be rewritten!"

2. Something is *possible* if there is a chance that it could be true.

LITTLE GIRL: Mom, is it possible the hospital switched me at birth and I'm really a princess?
MOTHER: Yes, but it's not likely. Now eat your asparagus – even a princess must eat her asparagus.

3. Something is *probable* if it is more likely to be true than not true.
   We must weigh the evidence in our minds and decide.

ANNOYED DAIRY FARMER: Dulcy got out of her pen again, and I can't find her – she's probably in Uruguay by now.
CALM WIFE: No, she always goes for my strawberries – that's where you'll probably find her.

If someone chooses to believe a possibility while continuing to ignore the evidence that supports an obvious probability, then he is using the possibility fallacy.

Our cure for this fallacy is to look at the evidence as if we had a balance scale in our hands. We look at the evidence, and we filter out the possibilities that are probably not true. This is hard for people like us! We never want to throw away our favorite possibilities. But we need to get this right – many choices in life can depend on judgments like this.

Exercises

A. In the examples below, indicate whether what is said is (1) totally impossible, (2) possibly true, or (3) probably true. (No evidence is given; simply use your knowledge of history, science, or the Bible.)

1. Moses and King David were great friends. They often went out for a milk shake at Checker's drive-in.

2. Abraham Lincoln decided to grow a beard after a little girl wrote him a letter saying he'd look better with one.

3. The tallest mountain in the lower forty-eight states is west of the Mississippi.

4. IOWA FARM BOY: Mom! Dad was out plowing the cornfield, and the tractor almost fell in a new volcano that's forming out there! Call the fire department!

5. NASA's Opportunity rover has found evidence of water on Mars.

6. *The Thinking Toolbox* is actually a covert CIA manual used to send coded

messages to agents in Argentina.

7. Honeybees don't sting when they're foraging for nectar.

8. GRANDPA, WITH FOUR-YEAR-OLD GRANDSON ON HIS KNEE: When I was your age, I did mountain climbing. I remember the day I summited on Everest alone . . .

B. Choose whether A or B is the wiser choice based on the evidence in each story below.

9. ADVERTISEMENT: Invest in our lead teacups – this is how the super-rich protect their wealth! We know the price of lead teacups hasn't changed for two hundred years, but this is only a trick. We've studied the market, and we have secret information that the price of lead teacups will soon go through the roof!

a. I should invest because it is possible lead teacups will increase in value.

b. I should not invest because lead teacups will probably not increase in value.

10. "Mom, Terrance is back!" exclaimed the little girl. "Oh my, let him in! Let's give him some warm milk," Mother said. "Why, Mother, Terrance is missing the tip of his ear! It's horrible. He needs a cat bandage," exclaimed the little girl. Later, the little girl asked, "Mother, you know what I think? I think Terrance was abducted by aliens. That's why we couldn't find him for so long." Mother said, "Dear, I don't think so. Cats roam around sometimes, and I think that was what Terrance was doing." The little girl didn't agree, "But don't you see it's possible Terrance was abducted? The aliens might have done an experiment on him and cut off the tip of his ear. That's what I think happened. I'm going to write a story about it and submit it to *Readers' Digest*. If Terrance could only speak to us . . . I wonder what he'd say."

a. MOTHER: I think you should stop reading those science fiction novels.

b. TERRANCE: They told me to take them to my leader. They're right outside the front door and they want to meet you.

Lesson 20

Circumstantial Evidence

If Constable Dobson arrives at a scene and sees a revolver, an upset chair, and a bloodstain on a victim's shirt, he is looking at *circumstantial evidence*.

Circumstantial evidence *is evidence which does not come directly from an eyewitness or participant and which requires some reasoning to figure out what it means.*

Constable Dobson is called in to investigate a crime. Lord Laudmoore lives in a two-story house in the country; he has a servant staff of one house-keeper and a chauffeur. This morning, he was found lying dead in his study. Next to him was a revolver with one chamber empty. Constable Dobson considers the gun to be circumstantial evidence.

Circumstantial evidence always requires us to use our thinking skills to deduce what it means. The revolver on the floor could mean some intruder shot Lord Laudmoore while he was sitting at his desk playing solitaire. Or it could mean Lord Laudmoore was enjoying target practice with the figurines on the mantelpiece when he had a heart attack and fell over dead. However, since a bullet wound was found on Lord Laudmoore, there is further circumstantial evidence pointing to a murder.

If Lord Laudmoore was known to keep a lot of money in his house, and if Seedy Sam, a local character with no money, was seen the next day buying expensive items at a shopping mall, this would be circumstantial evidence pointing toward Seedy Sam as a suspect. Maybe he murdered Lord Laudmoore and took his money.

But since nobody *saw* Seedy Sam murder Lord Laudmoore, the only evidence against him is circumstantial.

1. Rule for Circumstantial Evidence: *Circumstantial evidence can corroborate a witness's story by making it possible or probable.*

MARTHA THE HOUSEKEEPER: I locked up the house at 9:30 last night. I am sure all the doors and windows were locked. After that, I went home.

If after an examination, it was found that all the doors and windows *were* locked, and nothing had been broken into, we would have circumstantial evidence making what Martha the Housekeeper says possible, even probable. Therefore, Martha the Housekeeper's story is corroborated.

2. Rule for Circumstantial Evidence: *Circumstantial evidence can also show us whether an eyewitness's story is improbable or impossible.*

PINKIE THE VAGRANT: Yes, I know it was Seedy Sam who killed Lord Laudmoore because I saw 'im. I was sleepin' in da' bushes, like I always do, I was, when I sees this Seedy Sam come up with this long rifle in 'is 'and. Well I sees 'im come up to the window and then 'e shoots through the glass, see, then 'e throws the gun in the bushes and runs away.

From the circumstantial evidence gathered from the scene, Constable Dobson knows that parts of Pinkie the Vagrant's story are improbable, and other parts are impossible.

Pinkie says that the killer fired through the closed window; however Constable Dobson knows that no door or window in the house was broken into.

Also, Dobson knows that the murder weapon was probably not thrown in the bushes because, after searching, he found nothing. Pinkie's story, at best, is improbable.

1. **Circumstantial evidence needs to be interpreted in order to determine what it means.**

2. **Circumstantial evidence cannot lie; however we can interpret circumstantial evidence incorrectly.**

Exercises

A. During his investigation, Constable Dobson has collected these items of circumstantial evidence. Read this evidence carefully.

1. Lord Laudmoore was found dead early one morning lying on his study floor, shot through the heart. Next to him was found a .38 caliber revolver with one chamber empty.

2. Joe, Lord Laudmoore's chauffeur, who lives over the garage, reported the murder to the police.

3. After an examination, it was determined that Lord Laudmoore was shot with a .38 caliber pistol or revolver bullet at close range. The shot resulted in instantaneous death around 10:30 at night.

4. The window of the study (which was on the second floor) was locked. The rest of the outside doors and windows were locked, and nothing had been broken into.

5. One of the figurines on the fireplace mantel was shattered, and a .38 caliber bullet was found lodged in the wall behind the mantel. The

fireplace is next to the door.

6. Some fragments from the broken figurine were on Lord Laudmoore's coat.

7. Footage from a security camera near the front door shows a man identified as Dr. Radcliff leaving at 9:24 PM, and Martha the Housekeeper leaving at 9:31 PM. The camera recorded no other events that night.

B. Below are some eyewitness accounts. Based *only* on the circumstantial evidence given in the list above, choose whether the following eyewitness accounts are:

- PROBABLY TRUE (There is evidence which supports the statement.)
- POSSIBLY TRUE (Evidence doesn't support or deny the statement but leaves it open.)
- IMPROBABLE (Evidence or common sense makes the statement unlikely.)
- IMPOSSIBLE (Evidence makes the statement extremely improbable.)

State which item of circumstantial evidence supports your answer.

1. JOE THE CHAUFFEUR: It was about 10:30 at night when I heard this very loud bang like a gun going off – very loud. I thought it was Sir Laudmoore shooting the figurines on his mantelpiece – as he sometimes does when he's in an ill mood – so I didn't think any more of it until this morning.

2. SEEDY SAM: No, I didn't shoot Lord Laudmoore through the window.

3. JOE THE CHAUFFEUR: I was supposed to drive Lord Laudmoore somewhere at 8:00 this morning. I was waiting for him, but he never came. At 9:00 I unlocked the house and went in looking for him. I found him in his study just like you see him now. Then I called the police.

4. DAVID MCLURE: Murdered, you say? That's bad! I was invited to his house last evening to have dinner. I remember there was a man named Doctor Radcliff there as well. I don't remember noticin' anythin' out of the ordinary. The doctor left around 9:30 and I left around 10:00. Lord Laudmoore let me out.

5. JOE THE CHAUFFEUR: Maybe a shot from the Lord's gun ricocheted off the wall, bounced off the coal scooper, then came around and killed him? I've seen it happen in movies.

6. DR. RADCLIFF: Yes, I had dinner there last night. It was T-bone steak, that was the main course I believe – prepared by Lord Laudmoore's housekeeper, Martha. After dinner we talked for a while. A young man named David McLure was there as well. I guess Laudmoore had invited him. He seemed like a nice chap.

7. JOE THE CHAUFFEUR (INDICATING THE REVOLVER FOUND ON THE FLOOR): Yes, that is Lord Laudmoore's revolver. He normally kept it in his desk drawer.

8. MARTHA THE HOUSEKEEPER: That figurine must have been broken last night. I remember I dusted them yesterday afternoon and none were broken at that time. Lord Laudmoore breaks a lot of his figurines though.

9. What do you think Constable Dobson should do next?

Lesson 21

Puzzling Developments

Constable Dobson has been very busy since the last lesson. He has discovered:

- Lord Laudmoore's fingerprints were found on the revolver on the floor.
- The bullet found in the mantelpiece was fired from the revolver on the floor.
- The bullet in Lord Laudmoore was from an unknown revolver.

Meanwhile, Lord Laudmoore's sister, Lucille, has arrived, but she doesn't seem very upset.

LUCILLE LAUDMOORE: Oh, so he's dead, is he? I can't say I'm surprised. You see, my brother was a very selfish man – nobody really liked him. He was always scheming to get what he wanted – and would stop at nothing to get it. It seemed like all he ever did was collect these figurines; you can see them all over the house. I remember him once talking about one he particularly wanted – it was a statue of a boy with a long nose. He called it "Pinocchio." I don't know what he would do with it – probably break it. He would often buy figurines and then break them – or shoot them.

What should Constable Dobson do next?

"Constable Dobson should look more closely at David McLure, because he was never seen leaving the residence." – Denise F.

DAVID MCLURE: Me? Wh . . . why I only came over for dinner. Lord Laudmoore showed me his collection o' figurines, then I left; that was about ten o'clock. I hope ye aren't suspectin' me o' the crime. I hardly knew the man. I only met him at an auction. He invited me to his house to see some o' his figurines. I came over to see his collection, that's all. I left through the back door.

"Constable Dobson should question Martha about the presence of the two guests. What did they talk about?" – Susan F.

MARTHA THE HOUSEKEEPER: Goodness! I never listen through doors! That would be most improper. Besides, they didn't talk about anything interesting. Just the weather, figurines, and such. Mr. McLure had brought a figurine, and the Lord offered to buy it. Most boring. I would never care to listen to such boring conversations.

CONSTABLE DOBSON: Did Lord Laudmoore buy a figurine from David McLure?

MARTHA THE HOUSEKEEPER: Oh, I didn't say he sold it to him. Mr. McLure refused to sell. Lord Laudmoore came into the kitchen where I was lis . . . I mean, where I was washing the dishes, and he told me to take the rest of the night off. So I went home. Why he was so excited, I don't know. It was all probably very boring anyway.

"Constable Dobson should question Dr. Radcliff and Joe the Chauffeur on what they saw." – John P.

DR. RADCLIFF: Yes, Lord Laudmoore offered to buy a figurine from Mr. McLure last night. But because Lord Laudmoore told me to leave after that, I don't know if he sold it. A most rude fellow Lord Laudmoore is – telling his guests to leave before they've had dessert.

JOE THE CHAUFFEUR: I tell you, that old man was always conniving. Why, last evening, about ten o'clock, before I went to bed, I was looking out the window when I sees Lord Laudmoore come out of the back door and unplug the security camera on the back door, and then go back inside. He was up to no good, if you ask me.

Puzzling developments. But not as puzzling as . . .

CONSTABLE BLAKELY: Sir, you might be interested in seeing this. I found it in the bushes out back. It's a dinner jacket, with a bullet hole – here are powder burns. I took the liberty of looking at it closely, and as you can see, the laundry label says D. McLure.

    CONSTABLE DOBSON: Indeed, this just might clear things up a bit.

    LUCILLE LAUDMOORE: There it is! The Pinocchio! The one I was telling you about, there on the mantelpiece!

    CONSTABLE DOBSON: What! You mean the broken one?

    LUCILLE LAUDMOORE: Yes, see the long nose – just how my brother described it. That has got to be Pinocchio! I told you he would break it once he had it!

Exercises

A. Phew! We hope you have all those details down, because now it's your turn to solve The Mysterious Death of Lord Laudmoore. To help you out, we will offer two hints.

    1. HINT: Only one person is lying.
    2. HINT: The guilty one is the person who has a motive.

Here is what to do.

    1. Explain what happened last night in Lord Laudmoore's house. Explain who killed Lord Laudmoore, why, and how.
    2. Draw an opposing viewpoints chart. List some pieces of evidence which support your theory. List some pieces of evidence which weaken it.

3. Explain what Constable Dobson can do to help prove or disprove your theory.

When you are done with your assignment, find out how close you were. A long, complicated, and tedious solution to The Mysterious Death of Lord Laudmoore can be found in the answer key.

Tools for Science

Lesson 22

Mole the Scientist

Mr. Mole has lived all his life underground. But one bright day, he decides to crawl out of his tunnel to explore the world above. Remember, he has only experienced dirt, crawling, and grubby worms. This is important.

He ambles about – as moles are wont to do when they emerge into the sunlight. His toe bumps into a pebble on the ground. He picks it up and fits it in his mouth. Yuck, it doesn't taste like a nice mushy worm. He drops it, and it lands on his toe. That hurts.

Mole ambles on and meets another pebble. He picks it up. It doesn't taste any better than the first one. He drops it. That hurts.

Now Mole is no ordinary mole. He is an especially bright mole; he won first prize at the moleatorium for answering all the trivia on wormology. He forms a theory.

THEORY A: When I drop a pebble, it falls.

This may seem elementary, my dear Watson, but remember Mole's origin. Cramped tunnels are not a good place to learn what happens when you drop things on your toes.

Mole continues to amble. He discovers in his path a large snail hiding in its shell. He picks up the snail and tries to eat him. Can't get beyond the shell. Mole drops Snail. Now, what do you think Mole expects to happen? Nothing. Remember, Mole has no experience with dropping snails, only pebbles.

To Mole's surprise, Snail falls and hurts his toe. Mole reflects a moment. He is experiencing scientific thoughts.

THEORY B: When I drop anything, it falls.

Mole learns rapidly. He feels the grass beneath his toes; he sees the trees above his head. He stumbles upon Lady Beetle and picks her up. She draws her legs into her hard wing cases. So he drops her, but she doesn't fall; she spreads her wings and flies! Uh-oh, his theory must be revised!

THEORY C: When I drop anything, it falls, unless it is this particular Lady Beetle.

But this theory does not last long. Pretty soon, Mole discovers other things that fly. For instance, a dandelion puffball will just float away when you let it go – and sometimes it clings to you and refuses to let go.

THEORY D: When I drop anything that feels heavy and doesn't have wings, it will fall.

Thinking Like a Scientist

We should note what is happening in this story. Mole is acting like a scientist. He is trying to explain his observations in a useful way.

This is what scientists do:

DANGER
Multi-Tool
Science Gizmo

1. **Scientists invent scientific explanations which are useful ways of describing our world. These are also called hypotheses or theories.**

2. **Over time, scientists expand their explanations to include more and more things they observe.**

3. **Scientists learn a lot when their explanations turn out to be wrong – because even a bad explanation can lead to a better idea.**

This is what it means to do science. Science is something we all do. In these next lessons, we will show you how to think like a scientist.

Exercises

A. In the following examples, choose which are scientific explanations.

1. A sudden underwater movement of the earth's crust, called an earthquake, can cause a tsunami. A tsunami is a giant ocean wave which can travel 500 miles per hour, and when it reaches the shore, it can be over 50 feet tall.

2. I think it rains because the clouds become so heavy that they need to dump out some of their water or else they'll fall down.

3. MOTHER: I don't think I can go another night without any sleep.
   FATHER: If we put the baby to bed at a regular time, he might sleep

better.

4. I love you, Jane. Will you marry me?

5. JANE: I think you love me because you smile when you look at me.

6. "I know that [the Earth] is round, for I have seen its shadow on the moon." – Ferdinand Magellan, explorer, 1480-1521

7. Twas brillig, and the slithy toves did gyre and gimble in the wabe: All mimsy were the borogoves, and the mome raths outgrabe. – "Jabberwocky," by Lewis Carroll

8. SON: If you keep cutting the grass a half-inch high, you'll kill it. It doesn't have any leaves to grow back with.

B. In the following examples, chose the scientific explanation which best describes for you what is happening or what is being observed.

9. How many legs does this elephant have?

   a. This elephant is deformed and was born with five legs.

   b. This elephant appears to have five legs, but in reality it is an optical illusion.

   c. This elephant uses part of its trunk as a fifth leg.

10. BINGO: Mom, when I drink orange juice and milk at the same time, I get a stomachache. Why is this?

   a. MOM: Orange juice is orange, and milk is white. When you mix those two colors, they turn into a very sickly color. Would you like me to crochet a vest with that color for you?

b. MOM: Orange juice is an acid, and milk is a base. When mixed, they make a reaction that your stomach doesn't like.

11. BERT: I looked at the map of the United States, and it looks like most of the state capitals are in the middle of their states. Why do you think that is?

a. JENNY: Because each state wants to protect its capital from an attack by other states. If it is in the center of the state, it is harder to attack.

b. JENNY: Because if the capital is in the middle of the state, then everyone in the state has an equal distance to travel to reach it.

c. JENNY: That isn't true. The capital of Alaska is Juneau, and it is in the southeast corner of the state and doesn't even have any roads connecting it to the other parts of the state – the only way to reach it is by boat.

12. Choose which of the following theories best explains the time when the mailman arrives. The best theory is one which seems plausible and explains the most observations.

For the past two years, Guy Lombard has been keeping track of when the mailman stops at his mailbox to deliver his mail. Guy likes to get the mail as soon as possible because it is the only interesting thing that happens at his house. Guy has a theory: the mailman arrives anytime from 2:27 to 2:34, unless the weather is bad, in which case he might be up to an hour later.

a. The mailman arrives anytime from 2:27 to 2:34.

b. The mailman arrives anytime from 2:27 to 2:34, unless the weather delays him.

c. The mailman arrives anytime from 2:27 to 2:34, and every time the weather is bad Guy's watch goes bad and reads the wrong time.

13. Choose which of the following theories best explains Claire's allergy attacks. The best theory is one which seems plausible and explains the most observations.

Claire Annette has allergy attacks which last all day. She thinks she is allergic to her cat, Phuphu, who lives with her. But her attacks only happen once or twice a month in the spring and fall. When she has an allergy attack, she often sees Phuphu licking his fur, so she thinks this causes her sneezing. The vet told her that people are allergic to cats because they are allergic to cat saliva, and cats groom themselves year round. Claire bought an Elizabethan collar for Phuphu that is so big that he can't reach around it to lick his fur. However, now she thinks she's allergic to the collar itself because her allergy attacks haven't stopped.

a. Claire has allergy attacks because her cat licks his fur.

b. Claire has allergy attacks because her cat licks his fur, and she is allergic to Elizabethan collars.

c. Claire is not allergic to cats. She might be allergic to something in the air during the spring and fall, or she is allergic to something in her house she's not aware of.

References

We are indebted to Kenny Felder's article "Think Like a Scientist" for the inspiration for the example of Mole the Scientist (http://www.ncsu.edu/felder-public/kenny retrieved 3-30-2005).

Lesson 23

Tools that Help Scientists Do Their Job

Science is like a multi-tool gizmo. We can picture Bingo getting this gizmo for his birthday. Bingo might not know what he is holding and how useful it is. Bingo might realize only later in life that his parents have given him everything he needed to build something very dangerous.

Science is what builds airplanes, grows better corn, and helps us write logic books. Every tool on Bingo's gizmo has a use.

Science Tools

DANGER
Multi-Tool
Science Gizmo

1. **Observation** - Bingo keeps records and learns to use measuring instruments.

2. **Hypothesis** - Bingo brainstorms an idea that might help him solve a problem.

3. **Experimentation** - Bingo builds a test for his revolutionary idea - will it work?

4. **Analyzing Data** - Bingo finds out whether his test proved anything.

5. **Getting Advice** - Bingo asks other scientists to inspect his work.

In the next lessons, we will explain more about these tools and how to use them – without hurting yourself or blowing anything up. These are the tools of the scientific method. Everyone can use these tools to solve problems and answer questions because everyone does science, only some do it better than others.

Farmer Gray's Cow

Gray farms a dairy in central Wisconsin. He has a milk cow that won't eat – it is wasting away. Farmer Gray wonders if it is bad hay. Will he need to replace his winter hay? That'll cost way too much. He can't afford that.

Farmer Brown strolls over to offer his advice. He suspects a twisted stomach and suggests calling a vet. Farmer Gray gets irritated with Farmer Brown's hi-tech advice. And besides, vets cost too much. So when Farmer Brown is gone, Farmer Gray looks his cow "Buttercup" over. Buttercup doesn't have any strange bulges from her stomach being in the wrong place. That must not be the problem.

Farmer Judd up the road offers his advice. He once fed peanut butter to a cow, and it got its appetite back. Farmer Gray calls his wife on the cell phone, and she buys three quarts of Jiffer Peanut Butter. Farmer Gray feeds all three quarts to Buttercup with a giant syringe.

Two days later, Buttercup dies.

If Farmer Gray were a better barnyard scientist, his cows might have more confidence in him. How could science tools have helped Farmer Gray?

1. Farmer Gray could have simply fed one or two bales of a different kind of hay to Buttercup. This experiment wouldn't cost much.
2. Vets know a lot about cows. Cows know this. Just calling a vet to get advice would give Farmer Gray one more viewpoint to consider.
3. Farmer Gray could research Buttercup's symptoms in his *Farmer's Guide to Bovine Health*. He would have read that a twisted stomach, called a "displaced abomasum," does not necessarily produce any bulges.
4. Gray is tight with his money. He assumed a vet wasn't worth the cost. But losing a cow cost him much more. If he had spent $50 for a vet visit, he could have saved the $2,000 it cost to replace But-

tercup.

Farmer Gray sure made a mess of this situation. The rest of his cows might have something to say about this. For the animals' sake, farmers should listen up when they hear their cows say, "Science can help us if we use it."

Exercises

A. In the following examples, choose the science tool you think would best help the person in the example.

1. NATHANIEL: My Achilles tendon has started to hurt when I run. It started a while back. For years I've run in a pair of town shoes. That might have caused the problem. I bought a pair of new trail running shoes this week. My tendon still is a little sore when I rub it.

   a. HYPOTHESIS. Nathaniel needs to come up with a different explanation for his painful tendon.

   b. OBSERVATION. Nathaniel should pay attention to the way he runs to see if he can notice when it hurts and when it doesn't.

   c. GETTING ADVICE. Nathaniel needs to visit a foot doctor and ask him what to do.

   d. EXPERIMENTATION. Nathaniel hasn't waited long enough to see if the new shoes will take the pain away. He hasn't finished his experiment.

2. Marjorie was upset with herself. She had dropped a can of blueberry marmalade on her new cream-colored carpet. "Now, what did the carpet man say I should do with stains? He said to rub the whole rug down with whatever stained the rug. That way, it will all be the same color. Hmmm . . . I don't know about that." What should Marjorie do?

   a. OBSERVATION. Measure the size of the stain and it's proximity to the couch.

   b. GETTING ADVICE. Maybe look up "carpet stain removal" on the Internet.

   c. EXPERIMENT. Try removing the stain with lime juice mixed with hydrogen peroxide.

   d. HYPOTHESIS. Perhaps this really isn't blueberry marmalade. Maybe it's a deadly purple fungus.

3. Ebenezer is having trouble with his computer. Every time he tries to open up his favorite flight simulator, a message box pops up which says something. After he closes the message, his flight simulator won't open. What should Ebenezer do?

   a. GETTING ADVICE. Call the tech support people at the store and pay them $100 an hour to tell him how to fix the problem.

   b. EXPERIMENT. Try rebooting his computer and reinstall all the software.

   c. OBSERVATION. Read what the message box says when it pops up.

   d. HYPOTHESIS. "The last person who used this computer was my son, Tommy. He was messing around and arranging the icons on the desktop. He must have messed up the computer somehow."

B. Answer the following questions.

4. Name an experiment you've done – perhaps in the kitchen while cooking, in the garage on the family car, on your little brother that you shouldn't have, or someplace in your life that embarrasses you.

5. Is there anything wrong with this father's experiment?
FATHER: In a moment you'll see the world's best apple pie.
MOTHER: What does that mean?
FATHER: I've worked up a revolutionary new recipe for pie crust. We're out of butter, so I'm using applesauce.
MOTHER: Haven't I told you not to experiment?
FATHER: It's done. How does it taste? . . . Surely it's not that bad.
MOTHER: It is.

Lesson 24

How to Be a Keen Observer

How to Be Accurate

Have you ever climbed out of bed and the house felt like it was freezing, but after you showered, you stepped out of the bathroom and the house felt toasty warm? If you looked at a thermometer, you would notice that the temperature hadn't changed. What happened? Your senses told you the house felt warmer, but they were wrong. Your body warmed up instead.

Now, look at this illustration of two lines joined together with arrows.

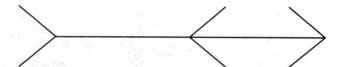

Does the line on the left look longer than the line on the right? You can use a ruler to measure each line if you like. This is an optical illusion. The angles make one line segment look longer than the other. The two line segments are actually the same length.

In these two examples, we used *measuring instruments* to overcome a fault in our senses. The thermometer and the ruler made our senses more accurate.

How to See More

Microscopes and telescopes also help our senses. Galileo was one of the first scientists to use a telescope. This is what he observed on January 7-8, 1610:

138

. . . when I was viewing the . . . heavens through a telescope, the planet Jupiter presented itself to my view, and . . . I noticed a circumstance which I had never been able to notice before, namely that three little stars, small but very bright, were near the planet; and . . . they made me somewhat wonder, because they seemed to be arranged exactly in a straight line. . . . When on January 8th . . . I turned again to look . . . I found . . . there were three little stars all west of Jupiter, and nearer together than on the previous night. I therefore concluded . . . that there are three stars in the heavens moving about Jupiter, as Venus and Mercury move around the Sun. – *Sidereus Nuncius*, 1610

Galileo was the first person to observe the moons of Jupiter.

There are many *scientific instruments* today that help us to observe things which our natural senses cannot see, including magnetic resonance imaging (MRI) to scan the inside of our bodies, and the Voyager spacecraft, which has sent back pictures of the planets.

How to Remember More

Have you ever woken up at night, looked at your digital alarm clock, and noticed that the numbers on the clock make a special sequence, such as 12:12, 1:23, or 2:22? A clock can only display a limited number of patterns like this. Why do we seem to wake up when there is a pattern, and not when there is no pattern? Many people believe this is more than a coincidence.

This is known as a *memory bias*. Our brain finds it easier to remember patterns. We forget things that have no pattern. Every time we wake up and see the numbers on the alarm clock and they have no pattern, our brain forgets all about it. Then we go back to sleep. Then when we ask our memory, "How many times have I woken up and seen a number pattern on the clock?" it replies, "Almost always!" But it is mistaken.

How do scientists overcome the problem of memory bias? They take careful and complete notes. They enter data into a database. They snap photos of their work. They keep a journal of their progress. They keep records of everything because they know their records may tell a different story than what they remember.

The Story of Pierre and Marie Curie

In the late 1800s, Henri Becquerel discovered by accident that uranium gave off strange rays that could darken a photographic plate.

Marie decided to make a systematic investigation of the mysterious "uranium rays." She had an excellent aid at her disposal – an electrometer for the measurement of weak electrical currents, which was constructed by Pierre and his brother, and was based on the piezoelectric effect.

Pierre Curie's electrometer

Results were not long in coming. Just after a few days Marie discovered that thorium gives off the same rays as uranium. Her continued systematic studies of the various chemical compounds gave the surprising result that the strength of the radiation did not depend on the compound that was being studied. It depended only on *the amount* of uranium or thorium. Chemical compounds of the same element generally have very different chemical and physical properties: one uranium compound is a dark powder, another is a transparent yellow crystal, but what was decisive for the radiation they gave off was only the amount of uranium they contained. Marie drew the conclusion that the ability to radiate did not depend on the arrangement of the atoms in a molecule, it must be linked to the interior of the atom itself. This discovery was absolutely revolutionary. *From a conceptual point of view it is her most important contribution to the development of physics.* She now went through the whole periodic system. Her findings were that only uranium and thorium gave off this radiation.

Marie's next idea, seemingly simple but brilliant, was to study the natural ores that contain uranium and thorium. She obtained samples from geological museums and found that of these ores, pitchblende was four to five times more active than was motivated by the amount of uranium. It was her hypothesis that a new element that was considerably more active than uranium was present in small amounts in the ore.

Fascinating new vistas were opening up. Pierre gave up his research . . . and joined Marie in her project. They found that the strong activity came with the fractions containing bismuth or barium. When Marie continued her analysis of the bismuth fractions, she found that every time she managed to take away an amount of bismuth, a residue with greater activity was left. At the end of June 1898, they had a substance that was about 300 times more strongly active than uranium. In the work they published in July 1898, they write, "We thus believe that the substance that we have extracted from pitchblende contains a metal never known before, akin to bismuth in its analytic properties. If the existence of this new metal is confirmed, we suggest that it should be called *polonium* after the name of the country of origin of one of us." It was also in this work that they used the term *radioactivity* for the first time. After another few months of work, the Curies informed *l'Académie des Sciences*, on 26 December 1898, that they had demonstrated strong grounds for having come upon an additional very active substance that behaved chemically almost like pure barium. They suggested the name of *radium* for the new element.

. . . Their laboratory was nothing more than a miserable hangar, where in winter the temperature dropped to around six degrees. One chemist commented that *"it looked more like a stable or a potato cellar."* And yet, Marie admitted that *"one of our pleasures was to enter our workshop at night; then, all around us, we would see the luminous silhouettes of the beakers and capsules that contained our products."*

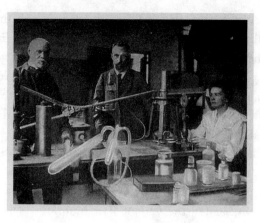

Pierre and Marie Curie with a friend in their labratory

How to Be a Keen Observer

The story of Pierre and Marie Curie illustrates what it means to be a keen observer. Before microscopes and telescopes, men and women had only their natural senses and their memory to study the world. Science made slow progress. Gradually, scientists found ways to make observations more accurate. In many ways, the story of science is the story of the instruments scientists have invented to observe the world.

So, is this lesson about using measuring instruments? Not exactly. Being a keen observer is more than the instruments we use – it is a habit we learn. It is a goal. Why were scientists motivated to invent instruments in the first place? Because they desperately wanted to be more accurate.

To be a keen observer:

1. **Learn to use scientific instruments to make accurate measurements.**

2. **Keep complete records of what you observe.**

3. **Observation is a habit – become a stickler for accuracy.**

Exercises

A. In the following questions, name a measuring instrument or method of keeping records which would help you to make these observations more accurately.

1. How much rain falls in one month at your home?

2. If you didn't have a timer, how could you tell if the cookies you are baking are done?

3. How many volts does an AA battery produce?

4. How many hairs are on your head?

5. How many seconds of difference is there between when the sun set tonight and when it will set one week from now?

6. On average, how much money does it cost per month to use the light bulbs in your room?

7. How much light does the brightest light in your home produce compared to direct sunlight at noon?

8. If you were color-blind, could you design a test for measuring how color-

blind you are?

B. Gather a group of friends or fellow students for the following activities.

9. Ask everyone to listen quietly for five minutes and describe on paper every type of sound they hear. Arrange to have someone make sounds outside the room, such as banging two objects together or popping balloons. After several minutes, ask each person to read his or her list. Did anyone hear a sound that no one else heard? Is it difficult to describe sound when you don't know what is making the sound?

10. Ask everyone to perform some task, such as putting together a jigsaw puzzle or playing a board game that requires everyone to pay attention. This is to keep everyone's attention occupied. Arrange to have someone walk into the room and perform a common task – such as sweeping up dirt or emptying the trash can – without attracting any attention. After the person leaves, ask everyone to write answers on paper to the following questions: What was the person was wearing? What color was his hair? What color was the broom he used? How full was the trash can he emptied? How long did he take to do his work? (You can also make up other questions.) If someone is unsure of what to answer, suggest they guess. Don't allow anyone to see what his friends are writing as answers. Next, bring the person back into the room and ask everyone to read what they wrote. Who was the most accurate? You may notice that some people remember things that are not true. For instance, they may remember the person wearing different clothes than they were really wearing. These are examples of memory bias. Sometimes our brain invents facts to help us answer questions we are unsure about.

11. Gather some objects ranging in size from an apple to a toy soldier or a piece of macaroni. Put these objects in a dark bag. Ask a group of friends to close their eyes. Hand one object around the group and allow each person to handle it without seeing it. Ask them to remember what the object feels like. Put the object back in the bag. Ask each person try to find that same object in the bag again without looking. You can use a stopwatch to time each person to see who can find the object the fastest. You are testing each person's ability to observe and remember what things feel like.

D. In these examples, explain what skills are being used and name a benefit each skill has.

12. Tea is made by steeping leaves of the tea bush *camellia sinensis* in hot water. Tea connoisseurs search for choice rare teas in the same way that wine and coffee connoisseurs delight in fine wines or coffee beans. Choice rare teas have complex aromas and flavors. Carefully cultivated, the best teas are grown on small farms at high elevations. Tea merchants purchase chests of this tea at auction. They hire a master taster to sample the teas. Master tasters have catalogued the many teas of the world by their taste and aroma. Only the best teas have an intense and distinctive flavor. A master taster can often remember clearly a cup of tea he drank years ago. He will close his mouth, hold the tea in the back of the mouth, swallow the tea and exhale through the nose, while keeping his mouth closed.

13. Agba lives in ancient Egypt. All his life he has seen his parents and other people look up at the sun to see what time it is. But every time Agba looks at the sun, it never tells him what time it is. Agba also notices that when two people agree to meet at the market place "at the ninth hour," often they show up at different times. He has found that if he looks at the length of shadows instead of looking at the sun, that the shadows are shortest in the middle of the day. He can use the length of shadows to gauge how much time there is before the sun sets. His friends are surprised by his skill, but they don't listen to him when he suggests they look at shadows instead of the sun.

14. Armand thinks his house is being invaded by large spiders. He's been trying to warn his mother about this. It seems like almost every time he goes downstairs in the middle of the night to get a drink of water, there is one on the sink or on the side of the refrigerator. His mother doesn't believe him. She says he is just experiencing memory bias. He is just forgetting about all the uneventful times he goes down for a drink of water and doesn't see a spider. He decides to keep a record of every time he goes down for a drink of water and whether he sees a spider or not. After two weeks, he shows his mother that he saw a spider eight times out of the ten times he went down. She agrees to call the pest control man.

15. Mr. Bascomb's job was to decode the secret message "LSLONP CJ

QNSQF KI AOJONSG PBONHSJ RNOO". The secret agent who gave him this job said the keyword might be "SEQUOIA." Mr. Bascomb remembered a code he had learned when he was a Boy Scout. It was called the Keyword Code. Each letter of the alphabet was switched with a different letter of the alphabet. He wrote out the alphabet.

ABCDEFGHIJKLMNOPQRSTUVWXYZ

Below it he wrote the code alphabet, starting with the keyword "SEQUOIA," and following the keyword with the rest of the alphabet, leaving out any letters which were already used in the keyword.

Row 1	A	B	C	D	E	F	G	H	I	J	K	L	M	N	O	P	Q	R	S	T	U	V	W	X	Y	Z
Row 2	S	E	Q	U	O	I	A	B	C	D	F	G	H	J	K	L	M	N	P	R	T	V	W	X	Y	Z

To decode the message, Mr. Bascomb must substitute each letter in the coded message with the letter in the alphabet that corresponds to it. For instance, the first letter in the coded message is "L." Mr. Bascomb finds "L" in Row 2 and then looks for the letter directly above it and sees "P." He then writes down "P" as the first letter in the decoded message. Mr. Bascomb translates the coded message as "PAPERS IN CRACK OF GENERAL SHERMAN TREE."

E. Read the following story and answer the questions below.

   Percival Lowell founded the Lowell Observatory in Flagstaff, Arizona. He was obsessed with the idea that an unknown planet was disturbing the orbit of the planet Neptune. After Lowell died, the observatory hired Clyde Tombaugh to search for "Planet X."

   Clyde found Pluto by taking many, many photographs with a special camera with a thirteen-inch objective lens built specifically for this search. He took two photos, two weeks apart, of each location in the sky where he thought "Planet X" might be. He then compared the stars in each pair of photos using an instrument called a *blink comparator* to see if he found any that moved – even slightly. On February 18, 1930, he found what he was looking for. Clyde became the only American ever to discover a planet.

16. Can you find the planet Pluto in these photographs taken by Clyde Tombaugh in 1930? Pluto is a very small dot towards the center of the first photo and disappears in the second photo.

Photo with Pluto   *Photo without Pluto*

References

The story of the Curie family was taken from "Marie and Pierre Curie and the Discovery of Polonium and Radium," a lecture by Nanny Fröman at the Royal Academy of Sciences in Stockholm, Sweden, on February 28, 1996, translation from Swedish to English by Nancy Marshall-Lundén. Used with permission. Visit http://nobelprize.org/physics/articles/curie to read the full essay. If you want to learn more, watch the movie *Madame Curie* (1943).

Lesson 25

Brainstorming

Brainstorming *is a process creative people use to invent an idea, find a solution to a problem, or answer a question.*

We are brainstorming whenever we spend time generating lots and lots of ideas that might help us to solve a problem. Here are some things with which brainstorming might help:

1. Decorating the bathroom
2. Generating ideas for a science fair project
3. Deciding where to go for your next vacation
4. Explaining why you keep having migraine headaches

Brainstorming can even be used to solve big problems, such as the problem of world terrorism.

MR. PRESIDENT: Okay, we're here to decide how to protect our nation from terrorists. Any ideas?

SEC. OF INTERIOR: What if we closed down all our national parks and monuments so the terrorists couldn't get in and hurt them?

SEC. OF TRANSPORTATION: And closed all the roads and ports so the terrorists can't get out.

SEC. OF ENERGY: But then I wouldn't be able to get to work in the morning.

SEC. OF LABOR: I think the best way to protect us from terrorism is to make it so the terrorists can't terrorize us. Does anybody agree?

SEC. OF EDUCATION: What about a contest for children from across the country to sew a big "Protect Us From Terrorism" quilt?

MR. PRESIDENT: Intriguing ideas. Does the Secretary of Defense have anything to say?

    SEC. OF DEFENSE: These donuts are good!

When brainstorming, not every idea has to be a good idea. In the President's brainstorm, most of the ideas were not good ideas. But the President should keep encouraging ideas until there is success.

1. Define the Problem

When you brainstorm, first you must define the problem you want to solve. Let's say you are going to enter a science fair, and you need a project idea.

2. Pick a Time

Next, you should choose a time for your brainstorm during the most productive time of the day. Good ideas often come in surges, so you should try to brainstorm when a surge is likely.

3. Encourage Ideas

Next, everybody should suggest ideas. The object in brainstorming is to produce as many ideas as we can. There should be no pressure on the brainstormers to make every idea a "brilliant" one. It is forbidden to criticize other people's ideas. Just because somebody offers an idea, that doesn't mean you have to do it (thank goodness).

    HANS: What should we write our article on?

    NATHANIEL: Maybe we could do it on the philosophical ramifications of the Platonian view of universal forms.

    HANS: You've been listening to those philosophy tapes too much.

    NATHANIEL: Brainstorming rule number three says you can't be critical of other people's ideas.

    HANS: I'm not being critical, just pointing out facts.

Often, brainstorming with a group of people is better than doing it by yourself because more ideas can be produced.

> BINGO: I want to do my science fair project on something I am interested in.
> DAD: You play a lot of paintball. What about doing something with that?

4. Write It Down

Assign somebody to be secretary. His job is to write down every idea so that good ideas will not be lost. This is a very important part of brainstorming.

> DAD: Here are the ideas we have for your science fair project: (1) How to make a paintball gun more accurate, (2) How to make it shoot farther, (3) What breed of guinea pig bites its owners the most? (4) How far do different kinds of rubber bands stretch before breaking? (5) Disproving Einstein's theory of relativity.
> BINGO: You forgot one idea: not doing a science fair project at all.
> DAD: That's out of the question.

While some of these ideas may seem impractical, it isn't always obvious you have found a good idea until later. That's why you need to write everything down.

5. Categorize

The next step is to categorize the ideas, perhaps improve them, and then decide which ones are the best.

Bingo and his dad could categorize their ideas under: "ideas involving paintballs," "ideas involving painful experiments," and "impractical ideas."

They could also improve some of their ideas. For example, "how to make a paintball gun more accurate" might change to "what factors reduce paintball accuracy?"

After categorizing their ideas, Bingo should wait a day before deciding which one is best. By then, one of Bingo's ideas may have matured into a really good science fair project idea. Remember, many great ideas started with a brainstorm.

SIR ARTHUR: I'm writing a story about a detective, but I don't know what to call him. Any ideas?

CHARLES: Is he smart?

SIR ARTHUR: Very smart. He can figure out everything about you just by looking at you – then he says it's "elementary." He can solve the most difficult of crimes with only minor clues. He can even break into a house without leaving a trace.

CHARLES: "Detective Watson" has a good ring to it.

SIR ARTHUR: Can't. I already used that name.

CHARLES: He can break into homes, you say. The other characters would do well to be sure they locked their homes.

SIR ARTHUR: Yes, they should be sure to lock their homes.

CHARLES: I have an idea . . .

DANGER
Multi-Tool
Science Gizmo

Define the problem you want to solve.

Brainstorm during a productive time of the day.

Write down a bad idea, then maybe everyone will start suggesting better ideas.

Use self-stick notes to write down each idea and stick them on the wall.

Exercises

A. Solve the following brainstorm problems.

1. The Smiths live in the country with a large acreage. Their dog, Suds, is kept in a pen at night and barks almost constantly all night. This keeps some of the Smiths awake at night – the ones sleeping on that side of the house. The Smiths want to solve the dog-barking problem so they can sleep at night. Brainstorm at least ten ideas which might solve the problem.

2. Farmer Gray has a problem with his cows getting out of the pen. He and his wife sat at their kitchen table and brainstormed. They were trying to find a way to keep the cows from getting into the strawberry patch. Which of the following ideas are not appropriate to put on the brainstorming list?

   a. Put bells on the cows so we can find them when they get out.

   b. Tie their tails together so they have to move as a herd.

   c. I don't think that would work. It would just make the cows upset.

d. Feed them hay by the barn so they don't want to leave.

e. Put up a fence.

f. We need to can some strawberry jam this spring so we'll have something to give away as Christmas presents.

3. Come up with a totally random series of words. Ten words.

4. The Smiths are still trying to solve Suds's barking problem. In the following conversation, which ideas either break a rule of brainstorming or should not be put on the brainstorming list?

a. Maybe we could all wear earmuffs at night, and then we wouldn't hear Suds barking.

b. That's a dumb idea. It would be very annoying to have earmuffs on while we are trying to sleep. They would fall off and roll on the floor.

c. How about keeping the dog in the house at night?

d. What do you think the dog is barking about? Perhaps we should figure out that first.

e. Maybe there is a skunk feeding out of the garden and he is barking at that.

f. Maybe we could leave him loose at night so he can kill whatever is causing him to bark.

g. We don't want to kill a cute skunk.

h. Maybe somebody could run out there tonight to see when he starts barking.

i. Maybe he is just barking at the moon.

j. We could move to Seattle where it's cloudy all the time, and then he wouldn't be able to see the moon.

5. Categorize the ideas in the previous conversation according to the type of idea.

6. Which of the ideas above do you think is the best idea?

Lesson 26

Hypothesis Is a Huge Word

What is the difference between a hypothesis and a brainstorm? Not much, really. They mean almost the same thing. Hypothesis is a big word that scientists use to describe an idea they create in a brainstorm.

Hubert never had hiccups before. Hiccups are a big deal to a hippo; every time he hiccupped, it sounded like a foghorn. His fiancée Hortense was annoyed. She suggested that they relax on the warm mud along the Nile and brainstorm.

HORTENSE: I think you hiccup because I'm so beautiful. It takes your breath away.

HUBERT: That's a dumb idea. When I hiccup, hooooc . . . I don't lose my breath, hooooc . . .

HORTENSE: Hubert, dear. The first rule in brainstorming says we aren't supposed to criticize each other's ideas.

HUBERT: Hooooc . . . maybe I hiccup because a piece of papyrus plant is stuck in my throat.

HORTENSE: I've heard that hiccups are caused by eating. Maybe you eat too much. You could go on a diet.

HUBERT: Hippos don't go on diets. That's it! My hypothesis will be, hooooc . . . "Hippos get hiccups because they don't have enough hamburgers"!

154

Have No Humongous Hypotheses

Forming a good hypothesis is more than coming to grips with a big word we don't understand.

A hypothesis *is an idea which we think will solve a problem or will answer a question.*

Putting our ideas into the form of a good scientific hypothesis will help us better understand our ideas.

There are good hypotheses and there are bad hypotheses. A good hypothesis is focused on one simple problem or question. It is simple, clear, and concise. A bad hypothesis is complicated or vague or tries to explain too much. It may contain words such as "all" or "never." The subject of a bad hypothesis is often hard to define.

DANGER
Multi-Tool
Science Gizmo

A good hypothesis explains a problem or answers a question in a clear, concise, useful, and testable way.

1. BAD HYPOTHESIS: "Something will happen in the future." Too vague.
   GOOD HYPOTHESIS: "Every day, ABC News reports at least one news event."
2. BAD: "Herbal remedies cure the common cold." Too broad. There are many herbal remedies; which ones are we talking about?
   GOOD: "Echinacea can reduce the symptoms of the common cold when taken before symptoms appear."
3. BAD: "7-Up tastes better than Sprite." Very subjective. 7-Up tastes better in whose opinion?
   GOOD: "Over 50 percent of my neighbors say they prefer 7-Up over Sprite."
4. BAD: "Mining for helium in the state of Iowa is difficult during the summer months because of the prevalence of mosquitoes, except

after a heavy snowfall, which the state of Iowa has never experienced in the summer but could if the polar ice caps keep melting." Not concise. There are at least two separate hypotheses here.
GOOD: "Mining helium in the state of Iowa is difficult because 97 percent of Iowa farmers refuse to allow scientists to dig up their fields to search for helium." And, "There is a 1 percent chance that the state of Iowa will experience a heavy snowfall during the summer months if the polar ice caps melt beyond their present size."

5. BAD: "Watching TV is not good." Not specific. In what ways is TV harmful?
   GOOD: "Watching eight hours of TV per day lowers some children's IQ by ten points."

6. BAD: "In World War II, the United States and Japan were at war." Not useful. This is common knowledge.
   GOOD: "In World War II, the Japanese attack on Pearl Harbor was a total surprise to everyone on the island, including Japanese spies."

7. BAD: "If a tree falls in a forest with no one to hear it, it makes no sound." Not useful. There is no way to test this hypothesis.
   GOOD: "If a tree falls in a forest when no person is within hearing range, and a digital recorder is placed near the tree, it will record no sound."

A poor hypothesis makes it difficult to use the tools of the scientific method. If we are not sure what we are testing, then we will have trouble designing an experiment to test our hypothesis. We'll have trouble making accurate observations because we don't know what we're looking for.

This is why we need to state our hypothesis using simple, clear, concise, useful, and testable terms.

Exercises

A. In the following hypotheses, decide whether each answers a question in a clear, concise, useful, and testable way. If it does not, create a better hypothesis.

1. This laundry detergent doesn't work.

2. It's cold outside.

3. This computer doesn't work.

4. Something's wrong with this car because I can hardly breathe it's so hot in this state of Texas.

5. Sugar makes children hyperactive.

6. Robert E. Lee was a really cool guy.

7. If I eat thirty ripe blueberries in less than one minute, then my mouth will turn blue.

8. All blueberries are blue.

9. All bears I have seen in this blueberry patch will also eat honey if I leave some out for them.

10. Banned pesticides like DDT can be found in 22 percent of the foods tested in 1999.

11. The South was right.

Lesson 27

How to Prove You Are Wrong

"That's what you have, a persecution complex," Bert said, leaning back.

"No, I just don't like to lose." Jenny moved her white queen two spaces to the left.

Bert blocked with his pawn. "You spend all your time finding ways you can lose? That takes all the fun out of it. I just try to win."

"Who wins more games? Check," Jenny said, lifting Bert's pawn off the board, replacing it with her white knight.

"That was a stupid move. I can just move my king," said Bert.

Jenny smiled, "Want to guess how many moves before I win?" She straightened her knight to face forward.

"No. I never like to think too far ahead."

Master chess players often search for ways their strategy might fail. In order to avoid mistakes, they anticipate their opponent's moves. This is good strategy.

Scientists use the same strategy. They test their favorite scientific hypothesis by trying to prove it is false. They look for experiments that may reveal a flaw in their reasoning. Most people find this difficult, but scientists have found it is very helpful.

Predict Something

A scientist begins by making a prediction. He asks himself, "If my hypothesis were false, then what would I see?" He will make a prediction from his hypothesis because it is impossible to test a hypothesis all by itself – a prediction is testable.

158

JENNY: Okay, our hypothesis is "The maximum altitude of a model rocket is determined by its weight." I predict that if a model rocket is launched with a payload, then it won't reach as high as if it were empty. If our hypothesis is false, then the rocket will reach the same height no matter what we put in it.

Bert and Jenny are using their hypothesis to predict something. If their hypothesis is false, then putting more weight in a model rocket will not change how high it goes. This seems like a reasonable prediction.

Test That Prediction

DANGER
Multi-Tool
Science Gizmo

Scientists test their hypotheses by asking themselves, "What is something I can predict, and how can I test this prediction?"

BERT: Too much payload might crash the rocket. I think we should just shoot our rocket without a payload. If it goes up high, we'll call it a success and stop. That rocket took a month to build.

JENNY: I don't see how this experiment proves anything. The science fair judge won't like it.

BERT: Oh, the science fair judge won't care. He'll think my rocket is cool.

JENNY: I think it would be better to shoot the rocket off several times. Each time we could use a bigger payload weight and we could measure how high the rocket goes. If the maximum altitude of the rocket does not decrease each time we increase the payload, then we will know there is a flaw in our hypothesis.

BERT: I guess. Maybe it would be fun to shoot the rocket off more times. We just have to be sure it doesn't get any scratches.

JENNY: But I think our hypothesis will turn out to be right. And I think the judge will like this experiment.

Bert and Jenny have succeeded in designing a good test for their prediction. A good prediction is one which makes it easy for scientists to test if it is true or not. Bad predictions are difficult to test. They can be ambiguous about what they are predicting, or they can predict something that is impossible to test.

> HANS: I think there are invisible pink rhinoceroses living in my room. They seize my rubber bands and guitar picks and eat them when I'm not looking. I predict that if I put a guitar pick in the middle of my room and watch it through the security camera, I will see an invisible pink rhinoceros eat it.

Hans's prediction is not a good one. It is impossible to see an invisible pink rhinoceros eat anything.

In the next lesson, we'll learn more about how to design a good experiment.

Exercises

A. In the following examples, which prediction would be easiest to test and would yield the most useful information?

1. In 1916, Albert Einstein published his paper on the "Theory of General Relativity." Einstein didn't expect everyone to believe him unless he could predict something using his theory.

   a. Einstein predicted that during a solar eclipse, astronomers should be able to see the sun's gravity bend starlight as it passed near the sun. If accurate photographs were taken with telescopes, the stars would show up in the wrong place. If the stars were not in the wrong place, then his theory would be falsified.

   b. Einstein predicted that in a few hundred years, his theory would allow scientists to design space ships which could travel above the speed of light. Einstein predicted that humans may someday colonize distant planets.

   c. Einstein predicted that if his theory were true and if the earth were to spin out of its orbit and go crashing into the sun, then most people on earth would die.

2. Nathaniel believes that Noah's flood was a real event and that air pressure before the flood was greater than today. He thinks this explains why fossilized plants are so large. His hypothesis is, "Plants grew better before the flood because of the greater air pressure."

   a. Nathaniel predicts that if he grows plants in a terrarium (a large glass bottle containing plants, soil, and water that makes a small ecosystem) and increases the air pressure, the plants will grow larger than regular plants.

   b. Nathaniel predicts that if he grows plants in a terrarium and removes almost all the air, the plants will not grow as well as plants in normal air pressure.

   c. Nathaniel predicts that he should be able to find fossilized plants which are larger than similar plants alive today.

3. Dewayne thinks diesel engines are more fuel-efficient than gasoline engines.

   a. Dewayne predicts that he should be able to drive a 2005 Volkswagen Touareg TDI diesel further than a 1995 Geo Metro gasoline before he runs out of fuel on the highway.

b. Dewayne predicts that if he drives a Mercedes-Benz E320 with a diesel engine for 5,000 miles, he will use fewer gallons of diesel fuel than if he drove a Mercedes-Benz E320 with a gasoline engine for 5,000 miles.

c. Dewayne predicts that if he looks up the EPA fuel efficiency rating of the Mercedes-Benz E320 with a CDI diesel engine, it should be at least ten miles per gallon better than the same car with a gasoline engine.

4. Dr. Bartlett has been hired to test a machine that packages raisins. It is supposed to package 1,350 to 1,470 raisins per box. The manufacturer wants to make sure the machine isn't putting too many raisins in the boxes.

a. Dr. Bartlett suggests the manufacturer wait to hear back from customers. He predicts that if customers complain, then the machine is malfunctioning.

b. Dr. Bartlett suggests the manufacturer open every box and count every raisin in every box – and then put the raisins back in the box.

c. Dr. Bartlett suggests the manufacturer select thirty random boxes from throughout the production day and count the raisins in each box. If the boxes contain 1,350 to 1,470 raisins per box, the machine is probably accurate.

5. Yuri loves soda. He thinks most people must prefer vanilla soda over cherry soda.

a. Yuri predicts that if he offers people the choice between a vanilla soda and a cherry soda, more people will accept the vanilla soda.

b. Yuri predicts that companies that sell vanilla soda make more money than companies that sell cherry soda.

c. Yuri predicts that if he drinks only vanilla soda he is less likely to catch the flu.

6. Tom wants to purchase a new rope for mountain climbing. He is looking at a lime green rope in a catalog. He thinks this rope will be strong enough to carry him and his gear across furious mountain streams and into deep mountain caverns.

a. Tom predicts that if the rope is as thick as his middle finger, then it will be strong enough.

b. Tom predicts that if he tries to cut the rope with a sharp knife, it will not cut.

c. Tom predicts that if he researches this rope on www.mountain-rope-reviewers-of-the-world.com, then lots of mountain climbers will say that this rope is a good one.

d. Tom predicts that if he ties one end of the rope to a tree and the other end to the bumper of his car, and he drives away from the tree, the rope will not break.

B. What is wrong with this example?

7. Doug's theory is that the United States suddenly came into existence in 1984 and that the government manufactured all the evidence that the United States existed before 1984 to cover up a conspiracy. He predicts that if you look at historical documents, they will say the U.S. existed before 1984, but they are lying. If you don't find any documents that say the U.S. existed before 1984, then his hypothesis is false.

Lesson 28

A Good Experiment

Sheriff Handy tipped his canteen – dry as dust. He must catch that horse thief soon. Thud! It felt like someone shoved a knitting needle though his shoulder. The outlaw had him where it hurt – no water, twenty miles to Chimneysmoke, and a dead horse. . . .

Hours later, Sheriff Handy's wound continued to bleed. He slumped in the shade of a cactus, pain throbbing though his mind. . . . "Juice from the cardón cactus can stop bleeding." Remembering this from a survival book, he sat up. He cut a piece of cactus with his knife and tied it firmly against the wound. "Worth an experiment," he thought, getting to his feet.

Sheriff Handy is experimenting with cactus juice. His hypothesis is "Juice from the cardón cactus can stop bleeding," and his experiment is designed to test whether this is true.

An experiment *is a way of testing a hypothesis – a way of finding out whether your hypothesis is true.*

However, the desert is not a good place to experiment. Sheriff Handy might be curious if the cactus juice will stop his wound from bleeding, but he won't learn much if it does. Why is this? If the bleeding stops, how will he know that the cactus juice did the job? The bleeding may have stopped on its own. He needs to compare his wound with a wound that was not treated with cactus juice.

A good scientist wants his experiment to:

1. **Have a single test variable.**

2. **Have a control, when possible.**

3. **Be repeated.**

Variable and Control

Sheriff Handy and the outlaw stood facing each other across the canyon. Guns empty, both were wounded in the shoulder.

"We can call this a truce," Handy said. "I can't reach you, and we'll both die if we don't reach town soon. God help the right man." Handy thought he saw the outlaw nod; he'd have to trust that. Turning, Handy started toward town.

Hours later, Sheriff Handy tied a piece of cardón cactus tight against his wound. "The outlaw likely won't know to do this," he thought, getting to his feet. "It's worth an experiment."

If Sheriff Handy's wound is similar to the outlaw's, and if Handy uses the cactus juice and the outlaw doesn't, and if he survives and the outlaw doesn't, then Handy will learn something. This is because a good experiment tries to compare two experiences to see if they are different.

A *variable* is a difference in something. In this experiment, the variable is the difference between Handy's wound and the outlaw's wound – the difference is the cactus juice that Handy used. We can call Handy's wound the *experiment* and the outlaw's wound the *control*.[1] Handy is comparing two wounds and how the single difference between the two wounds might change what happens.

To make a good experiment, Sheriff Handy needs to know there is only one difference between him and the outlaw. Both Sheriff Handy and the outlaw have the same wound, they are both in the hot desert, and they both have the same distance to travel back to town. The only difference – called the *variable* – is that Sheriff Handy used cactus juice.

If the outlaw had a canteen of water and Sheriff Handy did not, then this difference might change the results of the experiment. It might save the outlaw's life, but it would spoil the experiment.

Repeated Experiments

There is one more part to a good experiment.

> Many years later, the town of Chimneysmoke held a celebration for Sheriff "Cactus" Handy. Strangers were told the story of how "Cactus" had been shot five times while pursuing five different outlaws, and managed to survive each time by patching his wounds with slices of cactus. Someone suggested the Sheriff start a mail-order business selling cactus juice as a "cure for all ailments." "I just might do that!" the sheriff was heard to say.

There is always a chance that Handy overlooked something in his first experiment. There might be a coincidence – maybe it wasn't the type of cactus he thought it was, or the outlaw was only pretending to be wounded – and this skewed his results. So the more times Sheriff Handy repeats his experiment, the more likely he will notice any flaws, and the more confidence he can have in his results.[2]

Keep It Simple

Let's look at an experiment which failed and try to discover what went wrong.

> "You've suffered every morning for two weeks now," said Mrs. Little early one morning. "What can be causing these allergies?"
>
> Mr. Little moaned, "I'm bisderable. Don' dalk do be."
>
> Mrs. Little replied, "I've read some people are allergic to these Asian beetles in our house."
>
> "Baybe dad's id!" exclaimed Mr. Little. "Ged da vaguum zweeber!"
>
> Later that afternoon, Mr. Little reported, "It was the beetles. They're all in the vacuum, and my allergies are gone. The invasion has failed!"
>
> Next morning, he wasn't so happy, "It musbst nob be da beedles. I'b bisderable again."

When an experiment fails, often it is a good idea to look for some factor in the experiment which we weren't aware of – an unknown variable.

Mr. Little's hypothesis was that Asian beetles caused his allergies. He predicted that if there were no more beetles, and his allergies were gone, then the beetles must have been the cause. So he tested this by vacuuming up the beetles. The next morning, his allergies returned. Should Mr. Little conclude the beetles weren't causing his allergies?

If we read the description of what happened, we might notice something Mr. Little didn't notice. His allergies bothered him *every morning*. This might be an important factor. He should eliminate this variable.

> Mrs. Little observed, "I've noticed more beetles in the house in the morning when the sun shines on the east side of the house."
>
> Mr. Little replied, "You're right. Maybe they come in during the morning and leave in the afternoon. That's why I have allergies in the morning and not the afternoon." Later he announced, "Dear, I found a huge gob of dead beetles in the light fixture! That's where they're coming in! I've vacuumed them up and plugged the hole."
>
> Next morning, Mr. Little was happy. "This is the first morning I've felt like a human being!"

Experiments are tricky things. For us to learn something useful, we should be aware of factors that may influence our results. Keep it simple and you will build a good experiment.

Exercises

A. In the following examples, find the experiment that would best test the hypothesis. The best experiment is the one which (1) has a single test variable, (2) has a control, when possible, and (3) is repeated.

1. "I think winters in northern Illinois aren't as cold as they used to be."

   a. I'll ask Grandpa if he thinks winters are as cold today as they were when he was young.

   b. I'll go to the library and compare the meteorological records from the 1920s to the records for the last several winters.

   c. I'll count the inches of snow we had this winter.

2. "I think adding vanilla to this cookie recipe will make the cookies taste better."

   a. I'll add vanilla to a batch of cookies and taste them myself to see how good they are.

   b. I'll add vanilla to a batch of cookies and no vanilla to another batch of cookies and taste them myself to see how good they are.

c. I'll ask my aunt Martha if she thinks adding vanilla to cookies will make them taste better.

d. I'll add vanilla to a batch of cookies and no vanilla to another batch of cookies and have everyone in the family taste them without telling them which ones have vanilla and which ones don't. I'll ask them whether they liked the cookies.

3. "I think that there are invisible pink rhinoceroses living in my room. They seize my rubber bands and guitar picks and eat them when I'm not looking."

a. I will lay one guitar pick on the floor in the middle of my bedroom and watch it though a security camera until it disappears.

b. I will hire a cryptozoologist from the British Museum to examine my house for any signs of invisible pink rhinoceroses.

c. I will hire a big game hunter from Africa to hunt down and kill all invisible pink rhinoceroses in my house.

d. There really isn't any way of testing my hypothesis.

B. In the following experiments, find (1) the test variable and (2) the control, if there is one. If there is a weakness in the experiment, describe it.

4. Jenny thinks a grasshopper can jump farther than a cricket. She captures five adult crickets and grasshoppers. She places one grasshopper and one cricket on a line in the driveway and taps the ground behind them to make them jump. She repeats this with as many cricket-grasshopper pairs as she can get to do the trick. One grasshopper was disobedient and turned around and jumped on her head. She found that grasshoppers jump considerably farther than crickets.

5. The outlaw says he's quicker at the draw than Sheriff Handy. They are standing across the canyon from one another and Handy suggests the outlaw not test his hypothesis. "Why don't you just give yourself up and climb over to this side of the canyon. You'll get a fair trial." The outlaw insists he's quicker and pulls his gun. Roar! Guns spit and both men are wounded in the shoulder.

6. Miss Clarissa owns the best boardinghouse in Chimneysmoke. She is tired of caring for Sheriff Handy's shoulder wounds. She thinks this is a job for a wife and not an innkeeper. The Sheriff seems too distracted with catching outlaws to notice her caring work, so she decides to see if this is so. She'll demand he move to Mrs. Bambino's Cowpoke Corral down the street. She'll see if the sheriff notices the difference between her care and the rough care Mrs. Bambino dishes out.

7. Betsy is an easy target for new laundry products. She recently purchased two fabric softeners, SofStuff and LiquiPat – even though she's always been satisfied with Fabrix SF. The test is to see if her family notices any difference. She's been using Fabrix SF for several years now, so she decides to change to SofStuff for a month and then change to LiquiPat for a month. She will ask everyone in an unobtrusive way if they feel any difference in the softness of their clothes.

8. Dewayne is trying to decide between two diesel SUVs – the Jeep Liberty and the Volkswagen Touareg. Price is not a consideration; fuel economy is his goal. He suspects the Volkswagen will get worse gas mileage because it has a V10 engine. His plan is to ask the Jeep dealer if he can test-drive a diesel Liberty with an empty fuel tank. He will put two or three gallons of diesel fuel in and drive the Liberty until it reached the same empty point he started at. He will divide the number of miles he drove by the number of gallons he put in the tank. This will give him the fuel economy. Then he will go to the Volkswagen dealer and do the same for the Touareg.

9. Anna has played paintball for a month now and has shot her way to the top of everyone's respect. Anna wants to test paintballs to see which brand is better. She buys three different brands of paintballs, loads them into her Scorpion 007, and fires ten of each brand at a brick wall five feet away. Every paintball breaks. That didn't show much, so she fires the same number one hundred feet from a brick wall. All of them break. So she inflates an old air mattress and puts that in front of the brick wall. None of the Oucher brand break, and half of the Oucher Super don't break.

10. Nathaniel is concerned that extra-low frequency (ELF) electromagnetic radiation produced by power lines and power transformers may be dangerous. He builds a large coil magnet that he powers with ordinary

household current, thereby generating an electromagnetic field that fluctuates at 60 hertz – in the range of ELF waves. He puts a tray of dirt above this magnet and plants green beans in the tray. He also grows green beans in a similar tray far away from the magnet, but under the same environmental conditions. After several weeks, the tray near the magnet has very few bean sprouts, while the tray at a distance has many sprouts. He concludes that ELF waves are dangerous and presents his findings at the local science fair.

11. The Doctor [Ben Franklin], having published his method of verifying his hypothesis concerning the sameness of electricity with the matter of lightning, was waiting for the erection of a spire [on Christ Church] . . . when it occurred to him that by means of a common kite he could have better access to the regions of thunder than by any spire whatever. Preparing, therefore, a [kite], he took the opportunity of the first approaching thunderstorm to take a walk in the fields. . . . [H]e communicated his intended experiment to nobody but his son – then twenty-one, not a child as in the traditional illustrations of the scene – who assisted him in raising the kite. The kite being raised, a considerable time elapsed before there was any appearance of its being electrified. One very promising cloud had passed over it without any effect; when, at length, just as he was beginning to despair of his contrivance, he observed some loose threads of the hempen string to stand erect, and to avoid one another, just as if they had been suspended on a common conductor. Struck with this promising appearance, he immediately presented his knuckle to the key, and (let the reader judge of the exquisite pleasure he must have felt at that moment) the discovery was complete. He perceived a very evident electric spark. – an excerpt from Joseph Priestley's account

12. In 1847, Dr. Ignaz Semmelweis worked at the Vienna General Hospital. He was in charge of the First Obstetrical Clinic, where medical students helped women in childbirth. Records showed that 13 percent of women treated in the clinic died of puerperal fever. At the Second Obstetrical Clinic, operated by midwives, only 2 percent of women contracted the disease. Semmelweis was desperate for a solution. Pregnant women in Vienna were terrified to give birth in the First Obstetrical Clinic. They were afraid of dying – and for good reason. Both clinics were located in the same hospital and both used the same techniques. The only difference was the medical staff. Semmelweis observed that medical students

would walk from their classes in the autopsy room to their work in the maternity ward without washing their hands. However, midwives never visited the autopsy rooms. On a hunch, he ordered every doctor to wash his hands before entering the maternity ward.

13. Nathaniel hates getting sick. So he's trying to find a cure which nobody else has tried. He tries drinking water with colloidal silver in it to cure the common cold. He tries eating lots of echinacea root. When a cold settles in his voice box, he tries yelling at the top of his lungs to cure the hoarse throat. He tries drinking over a gallon of various herbal teas each day to make the flu end sooner than usual. He eats several large onions. He eats raw garlic bulbs. He tries not eating anything at all. He tries taking a very hot bath to cure the flu. He tries wearing gloves to town in order not to catch the cold. Nothing seems to work consistently.

C. Each of the following is a hypothesis. Describe a simple experiment which might test the hypothesis.

14. My dog likes eating dog food with milk better than dry dog food.

15. My sister is more likely to let me use her digital music player if I say "please" only once.

16. I can mow the lawn in less time if I edge it first instead of afterwards.

17. My family stays up later on weekends than weekdays.

Notes

1. This book introduces science at an informal level. Science terminology is complex and textbooks can disagree about the use of terms. We believe the terms we use are adequate for students and ordinary people to use in experiments around the house and for designing science fair projects – and this can be a springboard to further learning.

2. We are not talking about "repeatability" here. This idea is outside the scope of this book. We are recommending that experiments be repeated to eliminate hidden variables.

Lesson 29

How to Analyze Data

In the last lesson, Mr. Little removed Asian beetles with a vacuum sweeper and concluded that the beetles caused his allergies. Mr. Little had a problem, he hypothesized a solution, he tested his hypothesis, and the data was clear: "The beetles are gone and so are my allergies!"

If Mr. Little had repeated his experiment, he could have gathered more data. He could have gathered bags of beetles, spread them around the house, and watched whether his allergies returned, then vacuumed up the beetles and watched whether his allergies went away. Fortunate for Mrs. Little, he didn't think of this.

Analyzing data is one of the most difficult jobs for a scientist.

It is the future, and planet Earth is running out of helium-3 nuclear fuel. Captain Buz's mission: mine helium-3 from the moon. Lunar satellites and robots have returned a great deal of data. As we tune in, Buz is looking at this data.

BUZ: The whole earth is counting on us. We must move quickly.

SIDEKICK: Sir, your hypothesis is that higher concentrations of helium-3 may be found in the deepest lunar craters?

BUZ: Yes, Sidekick. But this data is so confusing!

Analyze Data

Data is information gathered by research or experimentation. Data can say four things:

1. "Good news - I support your hypothesis."

2. "Bad news - I don't support your hypothesis."

3. "No news - I'm ambiguous. I don't know what I'm saying."

4. "Mysterious news - I wasn't expecting to find this."

Good News

Some lessons back, we learned about being a keen observer. You may have asked yourself, "If I learn to use measuring instruments and keep records, what am I looking for?"

SIDEKICK: Sir, here are the graphs you requested.

BUZ: As you can see, the satellite readings of the lunar plains show helium-3 can be found in concentrations of 1.0-2.5 ppm [parts-per-million] in the dust. On Mons Hadley Delta, one of the tallest lunar mountains, the dust contains less than .0002 ppm of helium-3. However, robots have found readings as high as 15-20.5 ppm in deep craters.

Buz is looking for patterns, for common elements and trends in the graphs and charts. He's asking himself, "Does the data confirm my prediction?"

BUZ: The lowest readings are on the tallest mountains and the highest readings are below the surface of the moon. This seems to verify my prediction.

SIDEKICK: Should we risk landing an expedition?

BUZ: We boldly go where no man has gone before!

Things are going well for Captain Buz. But what happens when a scientist gets bad news?

Bad News

GRANNY: I can't download my e-mail. Could you fix it, honey? You're good at computers.

GRANDSON: Your SMTP driver might not be processing data packets. I'll update your MCRS32.

GRANDSON, *a few minutes later*: I updated your driver, but you're still not getting any e-mail.

GRANNY: Oh, you're such a dear . . .

GRANDSON: Maybe the firewall is blocking your e-mail. I'll turn that off.

GRANDSON, *a few minutes later*: I turned off the firewall, but you're still not getting e-mail.

GRANNY: You're being so helpful, I hate to bother you . . .

GRANDSON: Well . . . maybe the computer isn't connected to the Internet. I'll dial into the server again.

GRANDSON, *a few minutes later*: I redialed the server, but you're still don't have any e-mail.

GRANNY: I'm glad I have such a smart grandson . . .

GRANDSON: Maybe I could restart your computer.

GRANDSON, *a few minutes later*: I restarted the computer, but you're still not getting e-mail.

Sometimes it is easier to prove that something is false than to prove it is true. The grandson in this story has many hypotheses for why his grandmother can't download her e-mail. Each time he tests his hypothesis, he finds he is wrong. This can be very frustrating.

No News

It's worse, however, when the news we receive is ambiguous.

GRANNY: I think it's working now – here's a new e-mail in my inbox.

GRANDSON: Well, finally something worked . . . but this e-mail says it's from yesterday.

GRANNY: Oh, I think . . . I know . . . it wasn't here before, so the e-mail must be working.

GRANDSON: But your e-mail quit working this morning, and you checked it before it quit, right?

GRANNY: Yes.

GRANDSON: So this e-mail might have been here from yesterday, but you didn't notice.

GRANNY: I guess it could have . . .

GRANDSON: So we still don't know if your e-mail is working or not!

GRANNY: Oh, you're such a dear . . . maybe we should take a break and have some cookies.

Scientists do not like ambiguous data. This is why they design their experiments to give them a clear "yes" or "no" answer. They don't want vague results which could be interpreted more than one way. If the data is ambiguous, then scientists must look for unwarranted assumptions or errors and then do the experiment a different way.

Mysterious News

Another thing scientists can find is something they weren't expecting to find.

> *Captain Buz and his team have been mining helium-3 for a year. They are preparing to descend into the deepest crater.*
>
> SIDEKICK: No one has ever explored the Newton crater, sir. Let me check your powercell. You look frustrated, Captain.
>
> BUZ: We aren't finding the helium-3 we expected. Some places have it and some do not.
>
> SIDEKICK: Isn't your hypothesis that craters contain more helium-3 because they are protected from temperature changes. So why . . .
>
> BUZ: . . . Why do some craters have it and some don't? This data is ambiguous. Have you noticed how dust in some craters is marked with grooves? . . . I can't make any sense of this.
>
> *Sidekick's light illuminates the darkness as they descend . . . and as their boots sink into the ancient dust at the bottom . . . they stare in wonder.*

> SIDEKICK: It looks like a tractor, sir.
>
> BUZ: How can this be?
>
> SIDEKICK: I've been programmed to read all earth languages, and this writing is similar to ancient cuneiform hieroglyphs. It seems to say, "Property of Nimroz

the Great."

BUZ: This is why I became a scientist in the first place – to discover the unexpected . . . to boldly go where no man has gone before. . . .

SIDEKICK: I guess we'll have to go farther, sir.

Exercises

A. In the following examples, choose whether you think the evidence (1) tends to support the hypothesis, (2) tends not to support the hypothesis, (3) seems ambiguous, or (4) contains unexpected results.

1. Bert thinks gold is soluble in hydrochloric acid. He takes his 1933 Gold Double Eagle and drops it in a beaker of concentrated hydrochloric acid. Nothing happens.

2. Imagine you get a severe migraine headache at about 2:00 PM every other day. Imagine your friends suggest all sorts of cures for your migraines. You decide to try each suggestion for a week. Week 1, Jenny suggests you consume 100 mg of caffeine in coffee or pop when you feel a headache coming on. Week 2, Margaret suggests you take Ginkgo biloba herb extract every day. Week 3, Nate suggests you get four hours of strenuous cardiovascular exercise every day. On week 1, you experience one headache day; week 2, five headache days; week 3, three headache days. You conclude that the caffeine seems to work best.

3. Dewayne has been test-driving SUVs for the last seven months. He has a theory. Every SUV he's driven with eight cylinders in the engine got worse gas mileage than SUVs with six or four cylinders. However, he doesn't feel confident in his theory because he has only tested thirty-seven new and used SUVs on the market. He knows there are at least eleven he hasn't tested. He decides he'll try a new SUV made in Korea and another SUV manufactured between 1987 and 1991 in Moldova. He tests them and finds that the Moldovan SUV has four cylinders and gets just a little bit better mileage than the eight-cylinder Korean model.

4. You and your twin brother both came down with chicken pox at the same time. You want to get over the chicken pox very soon because your family is going on vacation. Your hypothesis is that sunlight will kill the

chicken pox germs, so you convince your twin brother to stay inside the house, while you sunbathe outside. He is very willing to do this because he feels miserable and doesn't understand why you'd want to get sunburn on top of chicken pox. The doctor says chicken pox lasts about seven days. You feel much better on the morning of the seventh day, while your twin brother feels better the morning of the eighth day.

5. Nathaniel has a lifelong fascination with conquering the common cold. He reads an article on how colloidal silver kills bacteria, so he builds his own colloidal silver generator. When someone in his family comes down with a cold, he takes some colloidal silver to strengthen his immune system. When he gets a cold, he takes even more. Sometimes he doesn't catch a cold, and sometimes the cold goes away in just two days.

6. Slovonov's hypothesis is that onion juice causes his eyes to water when it touches his hands. He decides to test this by chopping thirteen onions while wearing gloves. The gloves should keep his eyes from watering. He only succeeds in chopping two onions before he has to quit because his eyes are watering too much.

7. Sheriff Handy was thin, wiry, and short. Before the cactus incident, the Sheriff winced when people called him "Shorty." He was afraid the guys wouldn't think he was tough. His hypothesis was that if his nickname were "Cactus," the guys would think he was tough. If a memorable event involving a cactus was attached to him, people might call him "Cactus." He decided if he was shot in the desert by an outlaw, he'd use cactus juice on the wound, and then he'd tell everybody that the juice saved his life. As we all know, his scheme seemed to work.

8. There are 700,000 doctors in the United States, and they cause about 120,000 accidental deaths per year. This means there are about 0.171 accidental deaths per physician. Eighty million people own guns in the U.S., and they cause 1,503 accidental gun deaths per year. This means the number of accidental gun deaths per gun owner is about 0.0000188. Statistically, doctors are 9,000 times more dangerous than gun owners are. Guns don't kill people; doctors do. (Out of concern for our readers, we will not give the statistics on lawyers, because the alarm might cause you to panic and seek medical attention.)

9. Hans thinks that whenever his computer has an error message, it is

because an invisible pink rhinoceros has messed with it. He tests his hypothesis by sitting at his computer and waiting for an error message. When he gets one, he writes down whether he saw an invisible pink rhinoceros that time. After two months of careful observation, he has not seen a single invisible pink rhinoceros.

10. Your hypothesis is that Cleano laundry detergent works better than Dirt-go-way or Fresher. You test all three brands of laundry detergent by washing three loads of equally dirty laundry with each detergent. As a control, you also wash three loads without using any detergent at all. You discover that the load washed with no detergent at all is the cleanest.

Lesson 30

Listen and Learn

BINGO: I've got this idea, Dad. If I connect a battery to an electric motor, and have the motor turn an electric generator, and connect the generator to the battery so the electricity the generator produces goes to recharge the battery, wouldn't this setup run forever? The electricity would go in a circle, making more and more electricity! We could power our whole house this way!

MR. LITTLE: Son, I hate to disappoint you . . . but this has been tried before.

Imagine you are a serious scientist and you think you are about to discover something very amazing. But someone comes along and tells you he has already tried your idea. What a disappointment! But then you realize this saved you a lot of time.

Learning what others have done and listening to their advice can be the most useful tool of the scientific method – and the easiest to use.

Research

Scientists spend more time at the library than in a laboratory. Why do an experiment when all you need to do is read a book?

> BERT: I'm going to do my science fair project on my revolutionary idea that better light bulbs can be made by stuffing strips of paper into a glass tube and lighting them with an electric spark.
>
> JENNY: You might try reading about Thomas Edison's experiments with the light bulb. He found that tungsten produces more light than strips of paper do.

If a scientist has a question, he doesn't begin by doing an experiment. He reads books on the subject. He searches the Internet. He talks with other scientists. He is probably not the first person to be interested in this subject. Other scientists may have done experiments that he can build on.

DANGER
Multi-Tool
Science Gizmo

Research

1. **List the important terms and keywords related to your topic. Look these words up at a big library or on the Internet.**

3. **Keep copies of what you find in a notebook.**

4. **Look for two or more different viewpoints on your subject.**

If a scientist discovers that his question has been answered, he is happy. He can invest his time pursuing a different question. But if he doesn't find an answer, then it's off to the laboratory to start an experiment!

Peer Review

A peer is someone at your level. Your friends are your peers. A good scientist will ask other scientists to inspect his work to see if he missed anything. A good parent will ask for parenting advice. A good artist will invite his friends over to critique his sculpture. Authors of books such as *The Thinking Toolbox* send lessons to their friends for honest criticism. They want *peer review*.

You may have heard stories about reclusive scientists who discovered revolutionary ideas, but this is not how ordinary science grows. If we do our work in isolation, this isn't good science.

"A wise man will hear and increase learning, And a man of understanding will
   attain wise counsel" (Proverbs 1:5, NKJV).
"Listen to counsel and receive instruction, That you may be wise in your latter
   days" (Proverbs 19:20, NKJV).

When you ask for advice, don't be shy. Most people enjoy giving their opinions – especially scientists. Go to a college or university and talk to a qualified scientist about your question.

Peer Review

1. **Talk to your friends about what you plan to do. Ask if they have any ideas.**

2. **Interview an authority on your subject - like a teacher, historian, or doctor.**

Exercises

A. In the following examples, could the scientist have done a better job using peer review or research to reach his goal? How?

1. Bert couldn't think of a science project he wanted to do, so his mom told him to do one on crustaceans. Bert had never heard that word before, but he was too proud to ask what it meant. So he went to the library and asked the librarian where the section on "crust nations" was. She gave him a quizzical look and pointed to where he might find books on the lost city of Atlantis. He walked down the aisles, and the first thing he saw was a big picture book on World War II tanks. Cool. He sat in the aisle for an hour looking at pictures and trying to decide if he'd rather have a Sherman or a Tiger tank for his birthday. He photocopied a page about "thrust stations" and how the Germans used a technique called blitzkrieg to invade France. His Mom wasn't impressed.

2. Jenny was interested in too many subjects. She had to pick what to do her project on, and she chose crustaceans. She went to the Chinese buffet in town and asked the cook if he had any live crawdads he could spare. She smuggled these into a fish tank in her room and performed mysterious tests on them with an eyedropper and a sewing needle. She was afraid her friends might copy her work, so she hid what she was doing until the day of the science fair. When the lady at the registration table saw what was in her fish tank, Jenny was disqualified for breaking Rule 365(a) on the humane treatment of animals.

3. Howard had a secret he told to only a few friends. He knew how to build a perpetual motion machine! The idea was so simple that it was amazing that other scientists had never thought of it before. His machine involved magnets, and when he drew pictures of it, it looked like a huge crab. He said that if he ever built it, he would call it the "Crustacean Machine." He hoped someday to build a prototype.

4. Terra Turner never liked dark corners or tight spaces. She has no idea how her brother Terrance got her to go caving. Now she can't even see Terrance's feet. "That boy! How do you expect me to fit under this wet rock! What? Why is your voice echoing . . . wow . . . there's a room on the other side?" Terra wriggles a little further in the mud . . . and

. . . meets a cave cricket . . . looking at her. "Remain motionless," Terra thinks, as panic creeps into her mind. "Crickets are related to the crustacean family, and they are more afraid of me than I am of them."

5. Alberto Fujimori has always been interested in sand crabs. Since he lives on Oahu, Hawaii, he can go down to the beach and watch the crabs whenever he wants. For many months, he walks to the beach to observe crab behavior. Alberto talks to his neighbor Jacques Cousteau about what he is seeing, and Cousteau recommends he keep a notebook of his observations and take pictures. Alberto comes to some startling conclusions about what crabs do in their spare time, which he writes down in an essay and mails it to a friend of Jacques. He receives an enthusiastic reply and is flown to the National Institute of Water and Atmospheric Research, Wellington, New Zealand, for a conference on crustacean behavior.

Lesson 31

Pseudoscience

When someone says that what he is doing is scientific, but he does not use the tools of the scientific method and he tries to hide it, he is doing *pseudoscience*. Pseudoscience is fake science.

There is nothing wrong if we decide not to use all the tools of the scientific method. But we should be honest about this with ourselves and with others. The scientific method has a reputation for being reliable. We should not claim the authority of science if we don't use its tools. Pseudoscience is a form of deception. Sometimes people deceive others, and sometimes they deceive themselves.

ADVERTISEMENT: Indian Healing Salts are bringing refreshment to millions of stressed-out Americans. Discovered by Dr. Anyon Boyg on a research trip into the jungles of India, these salts have been used by native health practitioners for thousands of generations.

"My background in western medicine made me skeptical," said Dr. Boyg, "but the relief I've experienced from my ten-year battle with anxiety attacks made me a convert." (Dr. Anyon Boyg holds a doctorate in Magnetic Astrologics from BMI.)

Hindu lore has it that the jahjah, our body's healing center, can be thrown out of balance by our busy western lifestyle. Use of these salts, plus regular exercise, helps to rejuvenate the bioharmonic functions of our body. This may relieve symptoms of anxiety ten times better than the leading prescription medication.

Dr. Boyg is excited that he can make these salts available in America where they can bring new convergence to our stressful modern life. Now for only $69.99 you can . . .

Dr. Boyg uses many scientific sounding terms in this advertisement, and he tells us his medical credentials. He wants us to believe that his treatment has been scientifically tested. How can we tell if this is good science or not? We look for clues. We may find that an important tool of the scientific method is missing or that Dr. Boyg is doing a very bad job of using it. Some questions we could ask are:

1. Is Dr. Boyg making money from this? Scientists and doctors need to show they don't have a selfish interest in their claims. We need to be aware of biases.
2. Dr. Boyg says he is a doctor of Magnetic Astrologics. This term sounds very scientific, but what does it mean? He says he has a degree from BMI, but what do these letters refer to?
3. Does Dr. Boyg offer any scientific evidence to support his claim that Indian Healing Salts balance our "bioharmonics" – besides his personal experience? Has his product been tested by an independent laboratory?

Charlatan

Reliable Science

DANGER
Multi-Tool
Science Gizmo

1. **Pseudoscience ignores or misuses some science tools.**

2. **Pseudoscience always has an element of deception or ambiguity.**

3. **Pseudoscience is often promoted by someone with self-interest in the subject.**

On the other hand, here are some signs to look for in good science:

1. Good scientists are self-critical and admit their limitations. They do not exaggerate the value of their claims.
2. Good scientists explain how they used the tools of the scientific method. They do not leave us wondering.
3. Good scientists respect the opinions of scientists who disagree with them.
4. Good scientists are able to balance their excitement over new ideas with cautious skepticism.

These signs are not hard and fast rules. Many times, it is a matter of personal judgment.

Exercises

A. Read the following statements and examples, then decide if the example (1) is probably good science, (2) is probably pseudoscience, or (3) doesn't claim to be scientific. Explain your choice.

1. When I have a headache, I take aspirin. My doctor recommends it, and it seems to help most of the time. Maybe you should take aspirin for your headache.

2. My name is Joseph Goldman, and I've discovered an energy machine that could power the world. However, the oil companies have forced the government to refuse me a patent, so I can't show you how my invention works. I've watched all my ignorant science colleagues abandon me because they refused to acknowledge my revolutionary research.

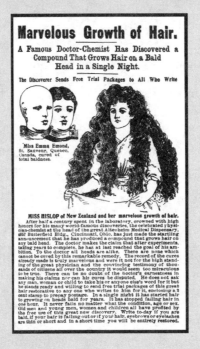

3. "Marvelous Growth of Hair" – After half a century spent in the laboratory, crowned with high honors for his many world-famous discoveries, the celebrated physician-chemist at the head of the great Altenheim Medical Dispensary, 4857 Butterfield Bldg., Cincinnati, Ohio, has just made the startling announcement that he has produced a compound that grows hair on any bald head. The doctor makes the claim that after experiments, taking years to complete, he has at last reached the goal of his ambition. To the doctor, all heads are alike. There are none which cannot be cured by this remarkable remedy. The record of the cures already made is truly marvelous and were it not for the high standing of

the great physician and the convincing testimony of thousands of citizens all over the country it would seem too miraculous to be true. There can be no doubt of the doctor's earnestness in making his claims nor can his cures be disputed. He does not ask any man, woman or child to take his or anyone else's word for it but he stands ready and willing to send free trial packages of this great hair restorative to any one who writes to him for it, enclosing a 2 cent stamp to prepay postage. In a single night it has started hair to growing on heads bald for years. It has stopped failing hair in one hour. It never fails no matter what the condition, age or sex. Old men and young men, women and children all have profited by the free use of this great new discovery. Write to-day if you are bald, if your hair is falling out or if your hair, eyebrows or eyelashes are thin or short and in a short time you will be entirely restored.

4. EDNA: The bathroom scale must be way off. I weighed 110 pounds when we were married, and I don't think I've changed much in thirty years. And at the doctor's office, I was wearing heavy shoes and a coat. Their scale had to be off by at least 40 pounds! I'd feel different if I'd gained that much weight!

5. Be careful about reading health books. You may die of a misprint.
   – Mark Twain

B. Indicate whether you think the following may be an example of (1) scientists resisting a good idea or (2) scientists being skeptical of pseudoscience. Explain your answer.

6. After their Kitty Hawk success, the Wrights flew their machine in open fields next to a busy rail line in Dayton, Ohio, for almost a year. American authorities refused to come to the demonstrations, and *Scientific American Magazine* published stories about "The Lying Brothers." Finally, the Wright brothers packed up and moved to Europe, where they caused an overnight sensation and sold aircraft contracts to France, Germany, and Britain. (Taken from http://www.amasci.com/weird/vindac.html)

7. ABOUT GODDARD'S IDEA OF ROCKETS: "The whole procedure [of shooting rockets into space]. . . presents difficulties of so fundamental a nature, that we are forced to dismiss the notion as essentially impracticable."
   – Sir Richard van der Riet Wooley, British astronomer in 1936.

Lesson 32

The Little Project

This is the story of a family project. We want to put all of the tools of the scientific method together and show you how they can be used.

As we tell this story, you will need a sheet of paper to hide the answers for each exercise. The answers are in the text. Cover this page and slide the piece of paper down until you reach the word "Exercise." Answer the question in the exercise, and then slide the paper down to reveal the answer.

The Idea

It is the year 2020, and Mr. Little has quit his job at Consolidated Computer Corporation. Bingo is back from an engineering apprenticeship, and Bonnie says she'll help too. The project: Mr. Little wants to design a little computer.

Bingo asks, "So, Dad, where do we start?"

Exercise: What scientific tool would be good for starting a project like this?

"Brainstorm," Mr. Little says. "We need a productive brainstorm session – like when Mom makes us hot cocoa and we solve the problems of the world."

By suppertime, the room is cluttered with coffee cups and sticky notes, but everyone feels good about the project. Bingo has his legs propped against the wall. "So we all agree this computer needs to be revolutionary and something the consumers want . . ."

". . . And we're tired of these huge computers the size of a book," Bonnie finishes. "We're tired of using a keyboard. We suspect lots of people feel the way we do."

Mrs. Little comments, "So this brainstorm session has given us a hypothesis – it's given us a goal. This is a good start, but we need more than a hunch about what people want. We need hard facts."

Exercise: What is a tool for transforming hunches into hard facts?

"Experiment," Mr. Little suggests. "We could ask prospective customers what they think the ultimate computer would be today."

After a day of brainstorming, it's time for supper, but the Little family has a plan of action. Mrs. Little begins listing friends who fit the profile of their future customers, but Bonnie points out that Mr. Pringle across the street has managed a marketing company before. He might have some suggestions. They invite him over.

Exercise: When the Little family invites Mr. Pringle over, what tool are they using?

"Peer review," Mr. Pringle says enthusiastically, "is a good thing to have in a situation like this. You're starting on the right foot. Like I've always said, a bird in hand is like two under the bridges behind you . . . or . . ."

"Yes," Mr. Little interrupts. "But didn't you have some suggestions, Bob, for how we could conduct a survey? We have never done this sort of thing."

"Well," Bob Pringle mused, "suburban families and growing businesses purchase most new computers. You could go door to door to hear what people want, and you could talk to the information technology officer at a few growing companies to learn what sort of computer they're looking to buy."

The Littles do just that. A week later they have plenty of data on paper.

Bingo says, "I've talked to hundreds of people and I've heard many opinions. How are we going to find what this data is saying?"

Exercise: What should the Littles do with all of the data that they have gathered?

"Analyze this data – we can make graphs and look for patterns in the information," Mrs. Little answers. She and Bonnie read though the consumer opinions, list the most common opinions, and count these. In the end, they find that most consumers say they want a laptop that (1) is reliable, (2) has a keyboard, (3) has a screen, (4) has a pencil sharpener, (5) they can put in their pocket, and (6) they can talk to.

Mrs. Little rubs her forehead. "I'd say this does confirm our hypothesis, but at the same time it doesn't. What do you say Dad?"

Mr. Little replies, "I'd say our customers are pretty choosy. They want a keyboard and a pencil sharpener, but they want it to fit in their pocket. I quit my job at the company because they weren't open to new ideas. I suspect our customers would give up a keyboard and a pencil sharpener in exchange for the other things they want."

Bonnie observes, "Maybe the customers gave us a clue. They mentioned they'd like to talk to their computer. Dad, can we do that?"

Exercise: What is a good tool for answering this question?

"Research," Mr. Little answers. "Why don't we visit the University of Nebraska Library and spend some time on the Internet researching computer technology? We'll learn the feasibility of an audio user interface."

The Littles do just that. After some late nights and a lot of reading, they conclude their idea will work.

The Prototype

Bonnie's department is to emulate the human voice. She wants the computer to talk the way humans do.

Exercise: What tool would help emulate the human voice?

Observation. Bonnie uses audio technology to record and study how humans talk and understand each other. She works with her dad to design a neural network to recognize the subtleties of the human voice and simulate the brain's ability to understand language.

Bingo's job is to fold the large video screen that customers demand into a box small enough to fit into a pocket. His challenge isn't the internal computer components such as the CPU or the hard drive. These are made by other companies. He is shaping the LCD composite materials to fold together like an accordion. And when he's done, Bingo is concerned about durability.

Mrs. Little comments, "Dear, you're being too perfectionist! We have a deadline. I'm sure it's good enough."

Bingo replies, "But Mom, I don't know anything about what I'm doing! I am certain I've missed something."

Exercise: How can Bingo alleviate his worries?

Peer review and testing. Mr. Pringle suggests letting Robie their dog chew on one of the prototypes – if it still works after the dog test, it'll survive any abuse. A reluctant Bingo watches Robie chew on his work. But after a few hours, Bingo can't find any scratches. Bingo's confidence is up.

The End

The Little Computer Company is celebrating the sale of the first "Little Computer" with a picnic. A circle of friends and family sit around Mr. Pringle as he demonstrates his new computer. "Marketing this product will be harder than designing it! You might think about hiring me," Mr. Pringle hints. Mr. Little says he'll think about it.

Mr. Pringle holds up hands for silence. "A young lady appears on your TV screen. Out of her pocket she takes a little box. It slides open with ease. A warm fuzzy face appears on the surface. "Hi, I'm Herbal the Verbal Gerbil, and I love to answer questions! . . ."

Projects and Games

Lesson 33

Projects

If you have read all the lessons and answered all the exercises thus far in this book, your brain is probably filled with all kinds of information on the scientific method, opposing viewpoints, and the difference between an argument and a fight. This information is now sitting in the "Facts and Information Lobe" of your brain waiting to be used.

Your brain looks something like this:

FACTS & INFORMATION LOBE

However, if the information inside your "Facts and Information Lobe" is not used soon, it might be erased and the space filled with other information like "in 1793 Eli Whitney invented the cotton gin."

When you spend time studying textbooks or memorizing facts – like the ones in this book – you are only using one part of your brain. And when you use only one part of your brain, the information is not retained very well.

However, if you *use* the tools in this book by doing a project – such as a science fair or history fair project – you will be exercising more of your brain than just the "Facts and Information Lobe."

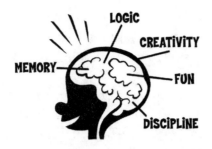

We want to encourage you to do a *project*. This could include:

1. Entering a local science fair or history fair.
2. Researching a question that interests you, such as, "Does the Loch Ness Monster exist?"
3. Writing a mystery and publishing it on the Internet.
4. Making a short movie.
5. Building a model rocket.
6. Starting a business selling things on the Internet.

A project is anything that interests you and has a goal in mind – such as building a nuclear particle accelerator or creating a better cookie recipe. While this lesson cannot tell you what project is right for you or how to do a project, we can give you a couple of hints.

Two keys to a successful project:

1. **What motivates you?**
2. **Start small.**

What motivates you? What are you good at? What are you interested in? If our mom had pushed us into entering the national spelling bee, not only would we have placed 873rd and 874th, but we would also have come away with bad memories. We needed something that motivated us.

We were motivated by:

1. Winning competitions with prize money.
2. Building something useful – like a model rocket.
3. Interest in a subject – like guitar, caving, or paintball.

Start small. A successful project doesn't have to be a big project. Don't begin by building an aircraft carrier. Start with something simple such as a history fair project on Queen Elizabeth. Enter a contest you might win. Research an easy question. Once your confidence is up, aim for something bigger – like running for president.

So, what now? We suggest you try out the next two lessons. After that, perhaps you could turn to Lesson 25 on brainstorming.

Lesson 34

"Herbal the Verbal Gerbil" Game

When you get tired of working on a project with your Little Computer, Herbal the Verbal Gerbil will suggest you play his game. "I'm going on a trip, and I want to bring some people with me. If you choose the right things to bring, I'll let you come. Name something you'd like to bring. You can name anything from an elephant to an eggplant . . . or even your aunt."

This game is fun to play in a group. One person is the traveler, and he or she is going on a trip. Everyone else takes turns guessing something which might qualify them to go on the trip. There is no limit to the number of things a person can guess. Everyone continues to guess until they get accepted. Once someone is accepted, he cannot name anything more.

The traveler is the one with the secret. He knows what things are acceptable and what things are not. No one else can know. The traveler does not accept the name of an object unless the first letter begins with the first letter in the first name of the person naming the object. For instance, if the prospective guest's name begins with an A, and he asks if he can bring an apple, albatross, annotated bibliography, afterthought, agate, or even the letter A, then the traveler says, "Yes, you can come along." If a prospective guest's name begins with the letter Z, and he asks if he can bring a salamander, Little Computer, myself, or even a Tyrannosaurus-Rex, then the traveler says, "No, you cannot come."

There are many versions of this game. The traveler can also accept (1) names of things that contain double letters, like coffee, or apple, (2) names of things that end with a vowel, like coffee, apple, or sea anemone, or (3) names of things that begin with the last letter in the word that was just previously guessed – but this last one is difficult.

This game teaches us (1) to be careful in observing the characteristics of each word, (2) to notice patterns in data, and (3) to develop a hypothesis and test it by naming words.

Lesson 35

The Mystery of the Large Letter Library

This mystery is a game. While one person can play it alone, we recommend you play it competitively with two teams. It will help to have more than one person on a team – it will not only make it easier, but it will also be more enjoyable.

A recent encyclopedia, *The Thinking Toolbox*, and a well-oiled brain are necessary to solve this mystery.

The Mystery

The Large Letter Library is housed in an aged building in the middle of the city. This library not only has a selection of ordinary fiction and nonfiction books, but it is also famous for its collection of rare and unusual books.

The Large Letter Library has four floors. On the first floor is the Department of Factual and Fabricated Facts, which includes all the nonfiction books. On the second floor is the Department of Long and Laborious Literature, which includes all the fiction. The third floor contains the Department of Actual Artful Artifacts, which is where rare and decaying books are protected. The fourth floor holds the Department of Miscellaneous Things, which contains all the items which would not fit in other places.

Yesterday, a rare edition of Herman Melville's novel, *Moby-Dick*, was stolen. This book is very unusual because, while on the outside it looks like an ordinary library book, on the inside each page is made from the skin of a genuine white whale. For many years it has been in a glass display in the Department of Actual Artful Artifacts.

Your job is to find out:

1. **Who stole the book?**

2. **How did he or she carry the book away without anyone noticing?**

3. **Where is the book now?**

The Rules

1. If you are playing with two teams, one team can begin with clue number one and work their way forwards, and the second team can begin with clue number twelve and work backwards.
2. If your team is stumped by a clue, move on to the next clue. However, teams cannot work on more than one clue at a time. Teams can obtain information from any source they choose, including encyclopedias or the Internet. Children can ask their parents or teacher for help. Once a team thinks it has the solution to a clue, they should write it down for further reference.
3. Once a team thinks it knows the answers to all three of the above questions, it can look in the back of this book for the solution. If all the questions are answered correctly, that team wins. If the team is wrong on any of the questions, it loses.

The Suspects

1. Felicia works in the Department of Factual and Fabricated Facts.
2. Lucile works in the Department of Long and Laborious Literature.
3. Artice works in the Department of Actual Artful Artifacts.
4. Hewey works in the Department of Miscellaneous Things.

5. Lamont is the Library Director and works at the checkout counter.
6. Greg is the janitor.
7. Melinda helps Lamont at the checkout counter and brings in the books from the book drop outside.
8. Gluber visits the library almost every day. He likes to read novels, but only exciting ones that are not very deep.
9. When the intercom announced the theft, Suzy-Sue was in the Department of Fabricated and Factual Facts reading a book on bird-watching.
10. Jean-Claude was in the Department of Long and Laborious Literature, reading *Les Misérables*.
11. Frank was researching the best method of porcupine quill removal on one of the computers in the Department of Miscellaneous Things.
12. Garth is the security guard. He tries to act useful by darting around corners and scribbling things in his notebook.

The Clues

Clue 1

GREG THE JANITOR: I was cleaning up in the Actual Artful Artifacts room at 10:30 AM, and I know I saw the *Moby-Dick* book in its case then. It must have been stolen sometime past 10:30.

ARTICE: It was terrible! I was just returning from my lunch break. I came into the Actual Artful Artifacts room and noticed that the door to the *Moby-Dick* display was open and the book was gone. I think it was about 12:30 PM.

Clue 2

The name of the thief begins with the same letter as the name of the capital city of the African nation of Botswana.

Clue 3

Suzy-Sue, Jean-Claude, and Frank disagree about who stole the book.

Only one of them is telling the truth.

> JEAN-CLAUDE: I'm pretty sure Greg the janitor took the book.
> SUZY-SUE: Greg the janitor didn't take it.
> FRANK: It was Lamont.

From the following evidence, assess which of the three people above is probably the most trustworthy.

Jean-Claude and Suzy-Sue are friends. Frank says Suzy-Sue is lying. Suzy-Sue says she is friends with Jean-Claude, but she knows he is a liar. Jean-Claude corroborates that Suzy-Sue cannot be trusted. But circumstantial evidence shows us that Jean-Claude is a liar. This means that Jean-Claude can't be trusted. Frank has a strong reason to lie.

Clue 4

The following clue is a series of multiple-choice questions. Choose the letter or letters which are before the correct answer in each question, then put the letters together to gain a clue for where the *Moby-Dick* book is now.

1. If you are traveling in a canoe and are attacked by a saltwater crocodile (*Crocodylus porosus*), which continent would you most likely be traveling in?
   on. Antarctica.
   r. Australia.
   c. Europe.
   r. North America.

2. In the book *A Christmas Carol* by Charles Dickens, the character Bob Cratchit was Ebenezer Scrooge's . . .
   th. Dead business partner.
   et. Clerk.
   a. Ghost of Christmas Past.
   em. Car mechanic.

3. The koala bear is a member of which group?
   t. Reptiles
   ur. Marsupials
   a. Calvinists

e. Bovines

4. During World War II, which country was never a member of the Axis?
m. Germany
t. Italy
n. Greece
q. Russia

5. How should you protect yourself in the event of an African killer bee attack?
bo. Run to the nearest water and submerge your body.
ab. Pull your shirt over your head and curl into a fetal position.
x. Never travel to an African country.

6. How should you find your way out of a dark cave if your light has gone out and you are alone?
d. Light your clothing on fire and use the light to find your way out.
q. Keep your hand against the wall to the right and keep walking until you eventually find the entrance.
x. Before you leave for the cave, tell someone where you will be going and how long you will be gone. When your light goes out, sit tight and wait to be rescued by properly equipped rescuers.

Clue 5

Look in Lesson 4, "Fact, Inference, or Opinion," for a clue. The person who is making an inference is saying something which is true.

Clue 6

The book is not BLAIR RYIN (unscramble the capital letters).

Clue 7

Look in Lesson 8, "When Not to Use Logic," for a clue. The person who is the most logical is telling the truth.

Clue 8

The book can be found lying between two books, *The Cloister and the Hearth* by Charles Reade and *One Hundred and One Recipes for Eggplant* by Clair Freeman. Where in or around the library is this possible?

Clue 9

GLUBER: *The Cloister and the Hearth* by Charles Reade is a depressing novel about the lives of two people who want to get married but cannot. I checked it out, but after reading a little bit of it, I found it exceedingly boring and depressing, so I returned it to the library this morning.

Clue 10

The following message is a clue. However, it is in code. Your job is to decode it. The coded message is "DEPRF YGY LMR REIB GR."

This is called the Keyword Code because you need a keyword to decode it. Your keyword is "EASY."

First, look Lesson 24, "How to Be a Keen Observer," to find out how the keyword code works, then come back here and decode your message.

Clue 11

The first letter of the first name of the thief is the same as the first letter in the first name of the first President of the United States.

Clue 12

GARTH: I'm sure the book was not stolen before 11:30 because I checked the rare book cases at 11:33 and nothing was missing then. See, I wrote it down in my notebook. I write everything down in my notebook just in case something important happens. I even wrote down the time the robbery was reported. See, it says, "12:30, Rare book noticed stolen out of glass case."

6

Answer Key

Lesson 1: A Thinking Tool

1. We would trust the librarian.

2. We wouldn't believe him.

3. We would believe him.

4. We suggest you ask Your Mortal Enemy to pick it up first.

5. Perhaps you should check one other book before picking up an Eastern tiger snake.

6. Derf doesn't think they are lost.

7. Answers will vary.

8. Pokerface Pete and The Kid both thought Rusty was the notorious criminal Deadeye Dan. They both tried to shoot him, and both missed. They shot each other instead.

Lesson 2: A Discussion, a Disagreement, an Argument, and a Fight

1. Disagreement.

2. Argument.

3. Disagreement.

4. Discussion. In the end, they didn't disagree on anything.

5. Discussion.

6. This might be a disagreement, but it is probably just a discussion. The Man With Big Hat said something, and Mrs. Oakley corrected him.

7. Disagreement.

8. Fight. They are not talking very nicely to each other.

Lesson 3: When It Is Dumb to Argue

1. Argue, if you have a good argument.

2. This is a pointless argument.

3. Argue your case.

4. Don't argue. The person obviously doesn't want to listen to reason or to the dictionary.

5. This is another pointless argument.

6. Run!

7. Yes.

8. Yes.

9. No.

10. No.

11. No.

12. No.

13. Presenting an argument, or might just be making an assertion.

14. Presenting an argument for everybody emptying their pockets.

Lesson 4: Fact, Inference, or Opinion

1. Statement of fact. We could verify this by comparing both books.

2. Bob is making an inference.

3. Statement of opinion.

4. Statement of opinion, or possibly statement of fact, depending on how it is meant.

5. Statement of inference made from facts.

6. Statement of opinion.

7. Statement of fact. This could be verified by examining a whale.

8. Statement of opinion.

9. Inference from observable scientific facts, or maybe opinion.

10. Statement of inference.

11. Probably a statement of opinion.

12. Statement of opinion.

13. Statement of fact.

14. Statement of fact. This could be checked by looking up city crime statistics.

15. A statement of opinion, or possibly a statement of inference, depending on why she thought it was on purpose.

16. Statement of fact followed by a statement of opinion.

17. Not warranted. The guy who isn't dead might have murdered the dead guy, and the dead guy shot back in self-defense before he died.

18. Not warranted. Bull elephants rarely gore people in saloons.

19. Warranted.

20. Not warranted. The teller was probably referring to the sheriff who would track him down and arrest him later.

21. Felice is stating a fact; Hewey, inference; and Lamont, opinion.

Lesson 5: Finding the Premises and Conclusion

1. Argument. Conclusion: I should eat my candy now. Premises: I might die before dinner. I might forget to eat it later. Grandma gave it to me to have when I wanted. I might have a stomach-ache and not be able to eat it.

2. This is a random series of sentences. Not an argument

3. Argument. Conclusion: The earth is flat. Premises: My mother told me the earth is flat. We can all see it is flat. A ball doesn't always roll when we set it down, so the earth must be flat.

4. Not an argument.

5. Not an argument. This is simply a string of conversation that is not intended to convince.

6. Argument. Conclusion: You don't love me. Premises: (1) If a man loves a woman, he buys her what she wants. (2) All women love flowers. (3) You didn't buy me flowers.

7. Argument. Conclusion: Midwestern towns are good places to live. Premise: They're safe because you know everyone personally.

8. Nathaniel: This may not be an argument. It is poetry written for literary effect. Hans: This is an argument and Nathaniel totally made this example up out of thin air.

9. This is a very foggy argument. The conclusion may be: Miss Madeline Bassett has something missing in the attic. Premise: Any girl who suddenly asks if the stars are God's daisy chain is a little off her rocker.

10. Argument. Conclusion: Philosophy is all a bunch of bunk. Premise: Philosophers can't prove anything they say.

11. Argument. Conclusion: The road commissioner is bad. Premise: He needlessly builds bridges. He is unlikable, etc.

12. Not an argument.

13. Argument. Conclusion: Slendra formula will make your family happy and help you lose weight. Premise: Slendra formula makes foods indigestible.

14. Argument. Conclusion: We could build a high-speed electric train. . . . Premise: A cat-toast combination would hover, etc.

Lesson 6: How to List Reasons Why You Believe Something

1. Nathaniel thinks he is a better foosball player because he moves his players quicker, he shoots the ball faster and he uses more energy. Hans believes he is a better player because he wins more games.

2. Lucy believes that Norma criticized her beekeeping business in a way that was unkind and that this justifies her revenge. Norma believes that honey is sticky, that she didn't say anything unkind about Lucy, and that she should apologize if she hurt Lucy's feelings.

3. (1) Columbus didn't fall off the edge when he sailed to America. (2) Astronauts have taken pictures of the earth from space, and it appears round. (3) Galileo proved the earth was round using math calculations. (4) Everyone knows it is round.

4. (1) If you look at the horizon, it looks flat. (2) Long ago, everyone, including scientists, believed the earth was flat. (3) If the earth were flat, it could be fun to look over the edge. (4) Near the edges, we could post "beware of dragons."

5. (1) Lots of people say it tastes good. (2) It has gobs of sugar in it. (3) It doesn't have any eggplant flavoring in it.

6. (1) Every Ford truck I've ever driven was great. (2) The farmer down the road swears he'll never drive another Chevy. (3) *Macho Truck Magazine* says Ford trucks can pull a 26,000-pound load, but Chevy can't.

7. (1) Sometimes it looks that way when it's a mess. (2) The alien world could look just like a bedroom and no one would notice.

8. A. Not a good reason. This is just a statement of what murder is. b. Good reason. c. Not a good reason. d. Some people believe this is a good answer, and others disagree because history records some cultures, such as the Aztec culture, that practiced ceremonial killing of innocent persons. e. Possible good reason. f. Possible good reason.

9. A. Possible good reasons. b. Good reason. c. Not a reason in itself. This simply rebuts an argument by those who believe the earth is flat. d. Not a good

reason. Bumps on a flat earth would allow rivers to flow. e. Good reason, as long as you knew the land was perfectly flat and didn't have any bumps or valleys.

10. A. Not a good reason. Beginners don't know much. b. Good reason. c. Good reason. d. Not a good reason. Movie actresses can be misinformed about honeybee behavior.

Lesson 7: How to Defeat Your Own Argument

1. This also means it is more difficult to climb the mountains. Also some people get altitude sickness in the Rocky Mountains.

2. Actually there is poison ivy in the Rocky Mountains. Also, if you stay on the trail you won't encounter much underbrush in the Appalachians.

3. This also makes the danger of avalanche greater. Being underneath a rock is very tedious and unenjoyable.

4. Mine shafts are dangerous. Falling down a mine shaft makes a

trip very tedious and unenjoyable.

5. Yeah, like mountain lions, rattlesnakes, and grizzly bears.

6. If the Bible isn't true, then we can ignore this reason.

7. How do you actually know they are feeling pain? They can't tell you anything. You don't really know.

8. I'm not so sure this is true. How can you prove that this was the case in all cultures around the world?

9. Well, I feel like it isn't wrong.

10. Yes, but the mother is alive as well. Doesn't that mother have the right to do what she wants with what is inside of her?

11. Yes, and that means they eat much more.

12. Yes, but they might bite the mailman, and then you would get sued.

13. Some people prefer floppy ears.

14. Yes, a smart dog knows how to get into trouble better than a dumb dog.

15. How do you know the book is telling the truth? Have you been in outer space to see it?

16. What encyclopedia? How do you know that the encyclopedia is not

lying? Maybe it's a vast international conspiracy.

17. I think it makes more logical sense to say Christmas comes in the wintertime everywhere in the world.

18. Ah, but more people live north of the equator than south of the equator. It would still be unbalanced.

Lesson 8: When Not to Use Logic

1. B is appropriate.

2. B is appropriate

3. B is appropriate. Joe probably isn't serious about Bob being color-blind; he's only being helpful.

4. C is appropriate.

5. C is appropriate.

6. C is appropriate – to those of us who don't like sheep cheese.

7. C is appropriate. Examples A and B do not answer the teacher's question.

8. C is appropriate. A cool head can save the day.

9. A is appropriate. There is only so much time in the day.

10. C is appropriate.

11. B. Hewey. Lamont does not make any sense at all.

Lesson 9: Using the Opposing Viewpoints Chart

1. Answers will vary.

2. Answers will vary.

3. Answers will vary.

4. Answers will vary.

5. Answers will vary.

6. They are opposing viewpoints.

7. They are not opposing viewpoints.

8. C, f, and h.

Lesson 10: Opposing Viewpoints Are Everywhere

1. Answers will vary.

2. Answers will vary. Possible answer: German shepherds are

not loyal; in fact, they often turn on their masters.

3. Answers will vary. Possible answer: Monarchy is a better form of government than democracy.

4. Answers will vary. Possible answer: Henry the Eighth was the best ruler England ever had.

5. Scientist Sedgwick

6. Bert. He isn't disagreeing with the other two; he is just pointing out a different fact.

7. Derf

8. Enrod

9. None. They each have a different point of view about the war. Hans disagrees with the other two by saying they shouldn't argue about it.

10. C, d, e (this is a circular argument), g, and j.

Lesson 11: The Good, the Bad, and the Ugly Evidence

1. C. Strong

2. C. Strong

3. None. No piece of evidence seems to stand out as strong or weak. Raymond doesn't have enough information to make a smart decision – assuming robbing a house could ever be a smart decision. Hopefully the Pringles' security measures will work.

Lesson 12: You Can't Believe Everything You Hear

1. If you don't know how a source obtained its information – how he knows what he knows – then the source should be considered unreliable.

2. We wouldn't.

3. I would believe him if I were you.

4. We wouldn't trust him.

5. If they know the facts already, why are they asking you? We wouldn't believe them.

6. We would say this is a reliable source.

7. B.

8. We wouldn't forward this. Since this e-mail says Microsoft's Web site has confirmed it, you could

check the Microsoft Web site.

9. We wouldn't forward this. You could visit KFC's website to see if they reference chicken. You could ask the University of New Hampshire to see if they did such a study. Or you could tour the KFC packing plant.

Lesson 13: Are You Primary or Secondary?

1. Because a story can change as it passes from one person to the next, a primary source is generally more reliable than a secondary source.

2. Probably a secondary source.

3. Primary source.

4. Secondary source.

5. Primary source.

6. Primary source.

7. Secondary source.

8. Sam is a primary source for what happened in the movie, but not for whether the movie is a true story.

9. Probably a secondary source.

Lesson 14: Who Has a Reason to Lie?

1. We should prefer the testimony of someone who does not have a reason to lie over someone who does.

2. No reason to lie.

3. Reason to lie. Bert wants to get Scotty to go to the movie.

4. No reason to lie.

5. Reason to lie. He wants to get the union behind the candidate.

6. No reason to lie.

7. Reason to lie. They sell gold themselves.

8. No reason to lie.

9. Reason to lie. He might want to become famous and be quoted in magazines.

10. Reason to lie. He sells the pills.

11. We would question this for reliability because we do not know where it is coming from.

12. No reason.

13. No reason.

14. Secondary source.

15. Reason to lie.

16. Nothing.

Lesson 15: Corroborating Evidence

1. The more corroborating evidence a source has, the stronger it becomes.

2. Corroborates Rusty.

3. This might corroborate Rusty, because Rusty was supposed to have robbed the bank alone.

4. Does not corroborate Rusty.

5. This corroborates Rusty's story, because this might indicate they were spending their loot.

6. Does not corroborate Rusty.

7. Does not corroborate Rusty.

8. Corroborates.

9. This does not corroborate. According to the story, alligators have lived down there eating rats for years.

10. Corroborates the fact that it might be possible, but not the fact that there are alligators in New York.

11. Does not corroborate.

12. Does not corroborate.

13. Does not corroborate.

14. Corroborates.

15. This author is involved with homeschooling himself, so he may be biased in his statement about homeschoolers.

16. No reason.

17. This is a secondary source.

18. He wants to sell the pills.

19. We would question this for reliability because we do not know where it is coming from or who is saying it.

Lesson 16: Mystery of the Stolen Manoot

1. Brinckley is a primary source for what he *did* see – Pinkie peeking in the window.

2. Brinckley seems to suspect Pinkie.

3. Brinckley has no known reason to lie.

4. The fact that Pinkie the Vagrant was found near the mansion in the morning supports Brinckley's testimony.

5. Answers will vary.

6. Mrs. McLeary is a primary source.

7. Mrs. McLeary may have a reason to lie. She may want to collect the insurance money.

8. Mrs. McLeary has corroborating evidence for part of her story – the forced window, the vagrant found on the grounds, and Brinckley the Butler.

9. She says that the man who stole her painting looked like a vagrant, but all she saw of him was his back, at night, and at a distance. Also, if she did see somebody running away from her house with a painting, surely she would suspect that her house had just been burgled. Also, the frame was found in the bushes, but her story seems to imply that the picture was still in the frame.

10. Answers will vary.

11. Mrs. Norton is a secondary source.

12. We do not know of a reason for her to lie – although judging from the way she speaks, it appears that she does not like Mrs. McLeary.

13. Mrs. Norton's opinion that Mrs. McLeary pinched the painting herself is supported by Pinkie the Vagrant.

14. Pinkie is a primary source.

15. He has a reason to lie; he is suspected of the crime.

16. The frame found in the bushes supports his story.

17. Some people might discredit Pinkie because he was a vagrant. We think this is unfair to Pinkie. However, he does have a strong reason to lie.

18. Perhaps the window area and picture frame should be dusted for fingerprints? Constable Dobson might want to check with the insurance company to find out about its insured value. He could search the house and grounds for the painting.

Lesson 17: Stir Plot until Thickened

Mystery of the Stolen Manoot: Conclusion

CONSTABLE DOBSON: Mrs. McLeary, I'm afraid I have some bad news.

MRS. MCLEARY: If it's about that dratted painting, don't bother.

CONSTABLE DOBSON: Uh, yes, as a matter of fact, it seems the thief has burnt it.

MRS. MCLEARY: Then he beat me to it. I was about to do it myself, if

I ever found it. I can't believe that swindler of an art dealer ever sold it to me. I have just heard the most shameful things about Manoot. I can't believe I ever liked the painting.

Do you know who stole the painting now?

"I think Brinckley the Butler did it. He has the best access to the fireplace/fires, aside from Mrs. McLeary, and his fingerprints were found on the frame and the window sill." – Kimberly

Constable Dobson went to talk to Brinckley the Butler again.

CONSTABLE DOBSON: Brinckley, it was you who stole Mrs. McLeary's painting and burnt it, wasn't it?

BRINCKLEY: Yes, sir. I must confess I am culpable in the matter. It seemed to me to be the best course in order to keep intact the prestige of Mrs. McLeary's collection. I also could not endure the daily task of viewing the painting for the purpose of dusting it. I took the steps you mentioned, planning to assuage Mrs. McLeary's grief by informing her later of the sordid details surrounding the origin of the painting. You see, sir, I am told Manoot was of the family Pongi-

dae.

CONSTABLE DOBSON: He was of the what?

BRINCKLEY: More specifically he was an orangutan, captured in the country of Borneo. I believe his owner had trained him to paint, and consequently made money off the animal by showing his talents in small villages on several continents. I have heard that this particular painting, *The Picnic*, was completed while on a trans-Saharan trek.

CONSTABLE DOBSON: Don't tell me he painted it while riding a camel.

BRINCKLEY: I believe that was the mode described to me. I also believe there were alcoholic stimulants involved as well, sir.

CONSTABLE DOBSON: Who would have guessed it? But Brinckley, what about Pinkie? Had he nothing to do with it?

BRINCKLEY: No, sir. I endeavored to cast suspicion on Pinkie in order to give Mrs. McLeary someone to blame, knowing she would never press charges. Also, the nights have been frigid lately, and I believe Pinkie finds it more comfortable in the jail. Will that be all sir?

CONSTABLE DOBSON: Quite. You may go.

BRINCKLEY: If I may ask, sir, will there be any charges filed in connection with the painting?

CONSTABLE DOBSON: I don't think so; I think the world has seen enough of *The Picnic* by Manoot.

The End

Lesson 18: Gunfight at the O.K. Corral

1. Yes.

2. He does not say.

3. No.

4. They were intending to leave town.

5. Yes. But he claims they did not give them enough time to surrender.

6. The Earps and Doc Holliday.

7. No. We know of no reason for him to lie.

8. The Clantons' side.

9. Strength: Mr. Gray has no known reason to lie. Weakness: We do not know how well he actually saw the gunfight.

10. He says Holliday fired first. He said their backs were to him, so he did not have a clear view. He has no reason to lie.

11. He says Holliday and Morgan Earp fired first. He had a clear view of the fight because he was involved in it. He has a reason to lie because he was on the Clanton side.

12. This seems to indicate that Virgil Earp tried to avoid a fight by giving a warning. He had a good view but has a reason to lie.

13. This seems to indicate that the Earps did not give the Clantons much time to surrender. From the way he describes the scene, he might not have had a good view of what happened. He has no known reason to lie.

14. Mrs. King seems to indicate that the Earps and Holliday intended to have a fight with the Clantons and did not intend to put much effort into disarming them first. She had a good view of what she saw. She has no reason to lie.

15. This seems to corroborate the fact that Ike Clanton intended to kill the Earps. But Virgil Earp has a reason to lie.

16. This seems to corroborate that the Clantons wanted to fight. Virgil does not have a reason to lie because he knows if J.L. Fonck could be questioned later to find out if he did say what Virgil claims he said.

17. This indicates that Ike Clanton

had it in for Holliday. However Kate Elder has a reason to lie because she was a friend of Holliday's.

18. Answers will vary.

Lesson 19: Does a "Possibly" Make a "Probably"?

1. Impossible. The Bible says Moses was dead before King David was born.

2. Probably true; there is strong evidence to support this.

3. Probably true.

4. Possible. It's always possible a new volcano will form in Iowa. It's more likely he ran over the gas pipeline.

5. Probably true. NASA is a reputable institution.

6. Possible.

7. Nathaniel: "Probably true." Hans: "Impossible. I've been stung in the eye by one of Nathaniel's bees when I wasn't near the hives."

8. Impossible. It is not reasonable that a four-year-old could climb

Mount Everest alone.

9. B. If the price of lead teacups hasn't changed for the past two hundred years, it's not likely it will today.

10. A.

Lesson 20: Circumstantial Evidence

1. Probably true. According to evidence #3, Lord Laudmoore was murdered at that time. This supports Joe's statement that a shot was fired then.

2. Probably true. Evidences #3 and #4 support this.

3. Possibly true. While we do know he called the police, we have no evidence indicating the rest of his story is true; it is only possible.

4. Improbable. Due to evidence #7, we know David did not leave through the front door, so he must have left through some other door. It seems improbable that Lord Laudmoore would have let him out a back door or window.

5. Improbable or impossible. The

physics seem a bit stretched here.

6. Possibly true, if we only consider the circumstantial evidence collected. But if we consider the testimony of David McLure, who says Radcliff had dinner with him that night, we can say this is probably true.

7. Possibly true. We have no evidence either way on this.

8. Probably true. Evidence #6 says that there were fragments from the figurine on Lord Laudmoore's coat, meaning the figurine was probably broken at the time of his death – this supports Martha.

9. Answers will vary. Perhaps Constable Dobson could ask Mr. McLure how he left the house, since he didn't show up on the front door security camera. Constable Dobson could dust the gun for fingerprints and find out what gun the bullet found in Lord Laudmoore came from.

Lesson 21: Puzzling Developments

The Solution

CONSTABLE DOBSON: It was you who shot Lord Laudmoore last night, wasn't it?

DAVID MCLURE: Yes, I suppose it's useless to hide it anymore. I shot him in self-defense. If I had not shot the Lord last night, I'm sure I would be dead instead of him. The man was about to kill me.

I had never seen Lord Laudmoore before yesterday. I met him at an auction, and he invited me to his house to see his figurine collection. He also sounded most interested in seeing my Pinocchio.

When I arrived, a Dr. Radcliff was there as well. I do not know his first name. We had dinner, and afterwards, Lord Laudmoore asked to see the figurine I had brought. I unwrapped it from a cloth and set it upon the table.

Lord Laudmoore became most agitated. He walked around to see it more closely. 'I will pay you a lot of money for this.' He offered me several times what I had paid for it.

As you may know, a collector buys, but never sells. And so I had no intention of parting with it. Besides, the whole situation seemed fishy. Lord Laudmoore had said he was also a collector, but he had no interest in the artistic qualities of my Pinocchio. He just wanted it. So I refused to sell.

After that, he sat for a moment with a moody look. I now know he was devising a plan. He rose and went into the kitchen, then returned and abruptly told Dr. Radcliff to leave. Dr. Radcliff was taken aback a bit, but seemed to take this rudeness well.

After the departure of Dr. Radcliff, Lord Laudmoore showed me about the house. His collection of figurines was not impressive. Many were broken and lying about. The whole situation seemed strange. He talked at random and repeated himself often. He would frequently glance out the window. Once he even excused himself and left the room for a minute. I don't know what he did.

Soon he became more insistent that I sell the figurine to him. He even left and returned from his study with a large quantity of bills, offering them to me in exchange for the figurine.

It was then that I perceived that the situation wasn't what it seemed to be. I resolved not to part with the figurine for any sum. 'Sir,' I said, 'I have no intention of selling this.'

'Ah, yes,' he said, 'just come upstairs with me and I will show you something which may change your mind.'

I carried the Pinocchio figurine with me as I followed him up to his study, which was upstairs and on the other side of the house. It seemed to me that he had taken me up to this room for some purpose, and I was wary. My thoughts were confirmed when, after entering, he calmly went to his desk and withdrew a revolver.

'I'm afraid, Mr. McLure, that the time for bargains has passed. I mean to have what is in your hand.'

This seemed to carry the thing a bit far, so I handed over the Pinocchio, it not being of that much worth to me. I asked him if I could leave, but he said, 'No, Mr. McLure, you must stay there for a moment.' There was something in the way he said it which told me that he meant to kill me.

Whenever I venture anywhere, I keep a revolver inside my waistband. This I took out, meaning to defend myself.

Both our shots went off at the same time. I do not know where Lord Laudmoore's went, but mine when through the Pinocchio figurine and straight into the Lord.

So there he lay on the floor, with fragments of the Pinocchio all over him.

My first thought was to escape the house. I admit my thinking wasn't clear. I had hoped the police would see the Lord lying next to his own gun, and conclude that he had used his own gun on himself. The only thing connecting me to the scene was the shattered Pinocchio.

I picked up the fragments and put them on the mantelpiece. My hope at the time was to remove every trace of the Pinocchio, it being a link to me and the scene. I hoped the maid would conclude that it had been broken before my arrival. Then I went downstairs and went out the back door, locking it behind me.

It was then that I noticed a bullet hole in the side of my jacket. I had escaped by a fraction of an inch – the bullet going through my jacket, but not through me. In a panic, I took the jacket off and put it deep in the bushes behind the house . . . foolish of me.

After that, I left. If I had been thinking clearly, I would have come straight to the police.

CONSTABLE DOBSON: This is a very interesting story. Since this is a case of self-defense, I do not believe there will be any charges. Why did Lord Laudmoore want the figurine so badly?

DAVID MCLURE: Perhaps he didn't want the figurine itself, but what was inside? . . . If you are done questioning me, I think I will go now.

The End

Lesson 22: Mole the Scientist

1. A scientific explanation for a tsunami.

2. Scientific explanation.

3. Scientific explanation. Father is suggesting irregular bedtimes might cause bad sleeping habits.

4. A question, not a scientific explanation.

5. Scientific explanation.

6. Scientific explanation that is now recognized as a fact.

7. Poetry, not a scientific explanation.

8. Scientific explanation.

9. B. It is more accurate to say this is an optical illusion.

10. B is an explanation, while A is not.

11. B seems the most reasonable explanation. It is unlikely that U.S. states are afraid of being attacked by other U.S. states. Also, Bert said most of the state's capitals are in the middle, not all of them.

12. B. This one explains the most.

13. C. It is unlikely that Claire is allergic to a collar.

Lesson 23: Tools that Help Scientists Do Their Job

1. D. He should run his experiment at least another week. However, other points on this list are also good. Answers may vary.

2. B. Getting some advice would be a good idea.

3. C. If he read what the message says he might get a clue as to why he can't open his flight simulator. The message might say something like "Please insert Flight Simulator CD."

4. Answers will vary.

5. Nothing is wrong. He had an idea, he tested his idea, and it didn't work. He'll know more next time. He could try mashed eggplant next time instead of applesauce.

Lesson 24: How to Be a Keen Observer

1. Use a rain gauge and keep a journal.

2. Poke a toothpick in the center of a cookie, and check how much dough remains on the toothpick when you remove it. Read in a cookbook how much dough indicates when the cookies are done.

3. Use a voltmeter.

4. You could count them, but you'd lose your place very easily. Divide your head into sections by marking it with a pen. Count the number of hairs in each section.

5. Find a precise way of determining the time when the sun has set and compare that time with next week's sunset time. You could also compare this with information from the weather radio.

6. Find out how much a kilowatt hour of electricity costs by looking at your power bill. Find

the total number of watts the lights in your room use – this information should be marked on them. Divide this number by a thousand to convert the watts into kilowatts. Then multiply this by the number of hours you use the lights and multiply this again by the cost per kilowatt-hour.

7. Use a photometer to measure the lumens.

8. No. You would not be able to know what colors you are not seeing. You need someone who is not color-blind to test you.

9. Answers will vary.

10. Answers will vary.

11. Answers will vary.

12. A master taster has a highly trained sense of taste and smell, and this helps him sort tea for tea merchants and tell them how valuable it is.

13. Agba is more accurately measuring the passage of time by measuring the length of shadows.

14. Armand keeps records to prove his memory is accurate.

15. Mr. Bascomb is using his ability to decode a message.

16. Answers will vary.

The arrow points to Pluto.

Lesson 25: Brainstorming

1. Answers will vary.

2. C and f

3. Answers will vary.

4. B and g.

5. Answers will vary. Ideas for finding out why Suds is barking. Ideas which do not involve stopping Suds's barking. Ways of directly stopping him from barking.

6. We think they should figure out what he is barking at first. Attempting to solve the problem before they know what is causing it might put them to a lot of bother which could be avoided. While putting the dog in the house or moving to Seattle might

solve the problem, it might also cause other problems.

Lesson 26: Hypothesis Is a Huge Word

1. Too broad. "This laundry detergent removes fewer stains than the laundry detergent I was using before."

2. Too vague. "The temperature outside this house is -34F."

3. Too vague. "This computer does not turn on when I push the power button, possibly because it is not plugged in."

4. Too broad. May contain more than one hypothesis, but it is hard to tell. "The air conditioner in this car is not cooling the air enough to make most people comfortable" and "Some people find it hard to breathe in Texas when the temperature is above 98F."

5. Too broad. "Children who are given large doses of sugar make more noise than children on a sugar-free diet."

6. Too vague. "Robert E. Lee was a good, just, brave, and honest

general."

7. Good hypothesis.

8. Impossible to prove. We would have to use a time machine to check the color of all blueberries that have ever existed. "Over 90 percent of healthy blueberries today are blue."

9. Good hypothesis, but dangerous.

10. The term "can be found" is too vague. "DDT can be found in one part per billion in 22 percent of foods tested in 1999."

11. Too broad and difficult to test. "Letters which Confederate soldiers sent home indicate that 53 percent of them had what I consider to be morally justifiable reasons for fighting against the Union Army."

Lesson 27: How to Prove You Are Wrong

1. A is easy to test. B can't be tested for many years, and C would be very expensive to test.

2. A would be the easiest to test. B is not good because decreasing the air pressure might kill

the plants. C would not tell us anything new because we already know there are fossilized plants that are larger than similar plants alive today.

3. C is easisest to test. B is also testable, but this would mean Dewayne would have to buy both cars. A is comparing two very different types of cars.

4. C is the best. A is not a good prediction because customers may not complain about having too many raisins. B is not a good prediction because the machine can fill boxes faster than raisins can be counted by hand.

5. A is the best prediction. B is testing the money a company makes, and this doesn't correlate well with how well people like vanilla and cherry soda. C is testing unrelated things.

6. D may be a good test, though it might hurt his car. C may also be a reasonable test – though it relies on other climbers' tests.

7. If you are a sane person and you strongly suspect Doug is mistaken, there is no way you can prove he is wrong! He's covered everything. Doug's theory is unfalsifiable – which means it is impossible to prove it true or false.

Lesson 28: A Good Experiment

1. B. The control is the meteorological records from the 1920s. The test variable is the temperature. Also, meteorological records are more accurate than a person's memory for events long ago.

2. D has a single test variable and a control. Every time someone in the family eats one of both types of cookie, more data is gathered.

3. D.

4. The test variable is the jumping ability of the crickets and the grasshoppers – that is what Jenny is comparing. There may be other factors that influence how far a cricket may jump. For instance, grasshoppers may jump further when something is tapped behind them, while crickets don't jump far until they become excited. Jenny might use different methods for motivating grasshoppers and crickets to jump. There is no clear control in this experiment unless it is the crickets themselves – sometimes no control is possible when comparing two things.

5. The outlaw was testing the speed of his draw compared to Handy's

draw. There was no control – we can't see how to insert a control without getting another person wounded. The sheriff hopes the outlaw won't feel the need to repeat this experiment.

6. The test variable is the difference between her care and Mrs. Bambino's lack of care. This isn't a very good experiment. There is no control that we can see, though she may be using her memory of the past as a control.

7. The test variable is the difference between the three fabric softeners. The control is everyone's subjective impression and memory of how soft their clothes feel. There don't seem to be any obvious flaws in this informal experiment.

8. The test variable is the difference in fuel economy between the two SUVs. He may be using the fact that each SUV is taken through the same regimen as the control, or he may use each vehicle as a control for the other vehicle. Dewayne did not repeat his experiment for a longer period of time. But this would be impossible without buying both of the vehicles.

9. The test variable is the different brands of paintballs. She is using each paintball brand as a control for the other brands. The flaw is that she wants to test which brand is "better." There are many factors that make a good paintball, including whether the paint color is easy to see and how many balls clog up the gun barrel. She needs to test these factors also.

10. The test variable was the presence of the 60-hertz electromagnetic waves. The control was the bean tray grown at a distance. The beans seeds near the magnet may have been defective, or there may have been poor water absorption in the growing medium. He should have repeated his experiment.

11. Ben Franklin wants to see if the storm cloud will produce any effects that are similar to electrical effects that he has seen in the laboratory. The test variable is the difference in the normal appearance of the kite string and what it looks like when it is under the storm cloud. The control is probably the normal appearance of kite string. There are flaws in this experiment, but it helped Ben Franklin move forward with his investigations of electricity. We're glad he was not struck by lightning because he hadn't yet signed the Declaration of Independence.

12. Once the doctors began to wash their hands (the variable), the death rate from puerperal fever suddenly dropped to 2 percent (compared to the control, which was the death rate in the time period before doctors washed their hands). Dr. Semmelweis's observations led him to discover the importance of hygiene. His work later helped Louis Pasteur.

13. Nathaniel is using a lot of different test variables, and he doesn't seem to have any control since he isn't certain how long his flu or cold will last with no treatment. He doesn't repeat his experiments enough over time to actually generate any reliable data.

14. Set out a dish of dry dog food and a dish of dog food with milk and see which one my dog eats first. Repeat this several times.

15. Ask my sister if I can use her digital music player and say "please" once. The next day do the same thing and say "please" twice. Repeat and record the results.

16. This summer, edge the lawn before mowing half the time, and edge it after mowing half the time, and record how long it took each time.

17. Each day, write on the calendar the time my family goes to bed. Analyze the results.

Lesson 29: How to Analyze Data

1. The data seems to falsify (not support) Bert's hypothesis. Bert probably should not have used his 1933 Gold Double Eagle for this experiment.

2. The data seems to support this conclusion. Caffeine seems to correlate the most with fewer headaches.

3. The data supports the hypothesis. Dewayne is testing gas mileage in relationship to the number of cylinders in an SUV, and his data shows a clear correlation between the two.

4. The data seems ambiguous. The doctor said chicken pox might last about seven days, which means you and your brother could have different recovery times. The sunlight may have helped, or it may not have helped.

5. The data seems ambiguous. Colds usually go away in a day or two, and often someone does not catch a cold even though his

family members do.

6. The data seems to falsify his hypothesis.

7. The change in nickname seems to correlate with the event involving a cactus. "Tough hombres will think I'm a prickly sort of fellow," thought Sheriff Handy.

8. If we assume the hypothesis is that doctors are more dangerous than gun owners are, then gun ownership seems to correlate with safety and doctors seem to correlate with danger. However, statistics like this often contain hidden assumptions. You shouldn't trust this sort of comparison unless you understand more about how this data was gathered or what data may have been left out.

9. This data is very ambiguous. There is no way to test for invisible pink rhinoceroses.

10. This data is surprising. Could it be that laundry detergent doesn't help to clean clothes? Maybe it's all a conspiracy of the laundry detergent manufacturers! You may decide to test this new theory.

Lesson 30: Listen and Learn

1. Bert should have asked his mom what the word meant. Crustaceans are in the phylum Arthropoda, which include shrimp and crabs. If you are unsure of what you are researching, then you should explain your problem to someone who might be able to help you.

2. Jenny should have shown her work to her friends to see if it complied with the science fair's rules. In order to receive the benefit of peer review, scientists must rely on the honesty of other scientists not to use their ideas without giving them credit.

3. Howard has no way of knowing if his idea has been tried before unless he is willing to put his idea before the scientific community.

4. Nothing about science here, but her research on cave crickets may be helping her overcome her fears. Terra knows she can just shoo the cricket out of the way and proceed with her caving adventure. Cave crickets are our friends.

5. Nothing wrong. This is good

research.

Lesson 31: Pseudoscience

1. Probably good science. He got advice, and he didn't exaggerate the benefits of aspirin.

2. Probably pseudoscience. Doesn't express respect for scientists who disagree with him. Doesn't give any evidence.

3. Pseudoscience. Very exaggerated claim, no indication of how research was conducted, and dubious statement of credentials.

4. Edna may not expect us to accept her claim as scientific, so she isn't deceiving us, but she may be deceiving herself. This is not good science. She is not using the "observation" tool. She is relying on her subjective impression of her weight instead of a scale.

5. Humor. Doesn't claim to be scientific.

6. Scientists resisting a good idea. A good scientist would not refuse to see evidence for an idea, even if he is skeptical.

7. This scientist is resisting a good idea. The fact that there are important difficulties with developing a new idea does not mean it is a bad idea. Goddard was an obscure scientist until 1944, when German rockets began bombing London.

Lesson 35: The Mystery of the Large Letter Library

1. The book was taken between 10:30 and 12:30.

2. Gaborone.

3. Suzy-Sue seems to be the most reliable because we know Jean-Claude and Frank cannot be trusted. ("Greg the janitor didn't take it.")

4. Return box.

5. The book either has been checked out or is still in the library.

6. In library.

7. The book is in or near the library.

8. The book is lying between a fiction book and a nonfiction book.

9. The fiction book was returned to the library by Gluber this morn-

ing.

10. "Garth did not take it."

11. George Washington.

12. The book was taken sometime between 11:33 and 12:30.

The Solution to the Mystery

1. Gluber took the book.

2. He saw the book in the case and took it. He didn't know he shouldn't take it. He then went to the checkout counter, and Lamont checked his book out for him without noticing what book it was.

3. He sat down on the bench outside the library and started reading the book. He was so bored by the first page that he decided not to read it. He put it in the return box.

About the Authors

Nathaniel and Hans live in the middle of a corn field, five miles from the Mississippi River, near New Boston, Illinois. They were home educated. They now spend their time climbing mountains, exploring caves, and writing books. You can pester them with questions on logic at www.christianlogic. com.

Acknowledgments

We would like to thank Sue Adams, Armand Aguiano, Chris Alexion, Mark Arndt, James Bartlett and family, Roslyn Bearchell, Brian Bosse, Ronda Clark, Johnny Eades, Dewayne Fender and family, Gabriella Flori, Christopher Freeman, Andy Fuzak and family, Leon Hedding, Lucas Hedding, Pete Hernandez and family, Caleb Heyden, David Hoffmann and family, Chris Hunton and family, Melissa Jones, Arlyn Kauffman, Mike Kline, John Lehmann, Calvin Lindstrom, Pat Marcum, Matthew McNatt, James Mieding, Kathy Muni, Jeremy Niednagel, John Notgrass, Joe Reynolds, Zack Reynolds, Jeff Royer and family, Jason Slafer, Adam Stanford, Ben Stegman, Cindi Topper, Toomas Vooglaid, Greg Wallace, Josh Welsh, and Toodles for their help in editing this book.

We would like to thank our parents and our sisters – without them we would never have begun this project.

The illustrations of "Toodles" the detective as well as the retro and western scenes are by Richard LaPierre, who transformed this from a boring book on logic into a thrilling cartoon adventure.

Our copyeditor was Mary Jo Tate, who has too much editorial clout to allow us to say anything about her.

🌼 Colophon

The book was designed by Nathaniel Bluedorn.
design.bloomingthorn.com

The fonts used were Adobe Caslon Pro
and Coop by House Industries.